John Codman

An American Transport in the Crimean War

John Codman

An American Transport in the Crimean War

ISBN/EAN: 9783743395794

Manufactured in Europe, USA, Canada, Australia, Japa

Cover: Foto ©ninafisch / pixelio.de

Manufactured and distributed by brebook publishing software (www.brebook.com)

John Codman

An American Transport in the Crimean War

AN AMERICAN TRANSPORT IN

THE CRIMEAN WAR.

BY
JOHN CODMAN
AUTHOR OF "THE ROUND TRIP," "TEN MONTHS IN
BRAZIL," "WINTER SKETCHES FROM THE
SADDLE," ETC.

INTRODUCTION BY I. C. ROPES.

NEW YORK
BONNELL, SILVER & CO.,
24 WEST TWENTY-SECOND STREET.

THIS LITTLE VOLUME

IS AFFECTIONATELY INSCRIBED

TO

MY WIFE AND DAUGHTER,

Mes Compagnons de Voyage.

TABLE OF CONTENTS.

	PAGE.
DEDICATION	3
INTRODUCTION	5
AUTHOR'S PREFACE	9

CHAPTER I.

The old and the new Mediterranean trade—The pioneer steamship—Arrival at Marseilles—The cholera—Origin of the Crimean war—French hilarity succeeded by disappointment.................... 13

CHAPTER II.

The passage to Constantinople—Reminiscences of antiquity—Ashore in the Dardanelles—Disinterested kindness of Suleyman Pasha—Constantinople and its surroundings—The passage to the Crimea—The seaports and the battle grounds—Starvation at the English camp—French economy and hospitality. 29

CHAPTER III.

The mistake of the Allies in making their landing—The commencement of the siege and the misery attending it—Another passage from Marseilles—Narrow escape from foundering in a gale—Arrival at Kamiesh—The Monastery of St. George...................... 51

TABLE OF CONTENTS.

CHAPTER IV.

The American and the French *cuisine*—A trip to the Sea of Azof—Contrasted scenes of peace and war—Vandalism of the Allies at Kertch—Trading with a Pasha —The unsuccessful attack on Sebastopol—Panic at Kamiesh and Balaklava—Return to Marseilles—Trip to Algeria.................................... 68

CHAPTER V.

Return again to the Crimea—Ravages of disease in the camps—French transport system compared with ours in the civil war—The Sisters of Charity—The capture of the Malakoff and Redan—A view of the ruins —Bomb-proof female curiosity................ 88

CHAPTER VI.

Entering the Turkish service—The Turk a man of his word—Good pay and little work—Our philosophic chief officer—The Pasha's bed-clothes—His friendship—No use for a propeller................. 112

CHAPTER VII.

Hafiz Effendi and his harem........................ 134

CHAPTER VIII.

Mustapha Pasha wide awake—We are hurried off to Eupatoria—A rescue in the Black Sea—A British frigate comes to our aid—Arrival at Eupatoria... 149

CHAPTER IX.

The blunder of a British General—A post-mortem held by Mr. Sears and some of his religious ideas—The end of the war and comments on its results..... 176

INTRODUCTION.

IT is with great pleasure that I comply with the request of my cousin, Captain John Codman, to write a few lines by way of an introduction to this entertaining narrative of his experience in command of an American chartered transport in the Crimean War.

That war was concluded forty years ago, and in the intervening period there have been four wars in Europe, three of them of great magnitude, and the other having been another contest between Russia and Turkey. It is probable that the Crimean War receives to-day but little attention from either historical or general students. But it is, in reality, a very interesting war, for it is the connecting link between the old and the modern systems of warfare. Not only by the substitution of steam for sails, and of iron for wood, is the change marked; it is distinctly to be perceived in the far more comprehensive and serious character which war has taken on since the days of the expedition to Sebastopol. Steam and iron are, in fact, but the symbols and illustrations of the spirit which dominates the nations of the present day, and insists upon the employment of every invention calculated to secure the greatest speed and the most unfailing certainty; in short, the most conclusive results in the employment of forces possessing far greater destructive powers than those known to Lord Raglan and General Todleben.

It is, however, to wars conducted on the old-fashioned scale and in accordance with old-fashioned methods that we must look for that element of picturesqueness in war which has always so powerfully attracted the imagination of mankind, and the Crimean War was the last of the picturesque wars of the world. It was, moreover, unusually rich in this element; the commingling of races, nationalities, religions and customs in the contending parties; the seat of the struggle, the Dardanelles, the Bosphorus, Constantinople, the Black Sea, with all their historical associations; the fact that, of the leaders of the contending armies, some had participated with distinction in the great Napoleonic wars of the early part of the century; these and similar things give to the Crimean War a character quite its own.

The narrative of Captain Codman is not in any sense a history of this war, but it is valuable because it contains the observations of a disinterested witness of many of the incidents of the struggle. And the story is told with a simplicity and naturalness, which, combined with the writer's genuine love of humor, cannot fail, I think, to make his modest contribution to the history of that period entertaining, suggestive, and well worth the attention of the public.

JOHN CODMAN ROPES.

BOSTON, December 1, 1896.

THE AUTHOR'S PREFACE.

I HAVE thought it opportune to publish this short narrative at a time when the Turkish question is so generally discussed by the press.

It is merely an account of events that occurred under my personal observation, with occasional references to their political significance.

No change to suit present conditions has been made from the original notes, taken upon the spot forty years and more ago. I have spoken of the Turk as we found him then, not as he is represented to be now.

At that time Christians of all denominations were protected by the government equally with the Mahomedans. The Armenians, on account of their superior intelligence, and greater aptitude for business than those of other sects, held offices of public trust, and many of them served in the army and navy.

Competent authorities agree that the treatment of Christians in general by the Turkish government has not changed from that time to the present, that out of a population of four million Christians, two millions of whom are Armenians, the proportion of officials is far greater than is that represented by all the Moslems in the empire, and that in ordinary civil life no distinction is made among the people because of their religious faith.

It must be evident, therefore, to any candid mind that the butcheries consequent upon dissensions in Asiatic Turkey from which the Armenians have suffered more than the Turks, because as contestants they are fewer in number, are attributable to other causes than that of religious persecution.

There is great danger, however, that the well-meant efforts of philanthropists may give religion a prominence in this controversy which does not belong to it. Once made a *casus belli*, either by armed interference or by intemperate words of diplomacy, the universal slaughter of Christians of all denominations would ensue from a general uprising of Mahomedans throughout Asia and Africa and the East Indian Islands, where they number more than 250,000,000, for it must be remembered that the Sultan is Caliph, and, as such, the head of the whole Mahomedan Church, as well as the despotic ruler of his own dominions.

The humanity that would prompt such inhumanity as this is as unchristian as it is impolitic.

This suggestion is commended to the reflection of my readers as of more value than anything else they may find in further turning over the leaves of this book.

AN AMERICAN TRANSPORT IN THE CRIMEAN WAR.

CHAPTER I.

IN the year 1854 the commercial marine of the United States was at the height of its prosperity. Steam had not at that time become to any considerable extent a factor in the carriage of merchandise, and the whole trade of this country with the Mediterranean was carried on in sailing vessels, and those almost universally under the American flag. Passengers who desired to visit the shores of that sea were obliged, unless they had the inclination, and time to spare to be wafted across by the white wings of the sailing craft of that day, to take a Cunard steamer for Liverpool, and thence to travel across England, the Straits of Dover, and the entire length of France, until they reached Marseilles. No merchant steamer from this country had ever passed through the Straits of Gibraltar. The feasibility of establishing a steamship line from New York to Gibraltar and Marseilles first occurred to the firm of N. L. McCready & Co., an enterprising shipping house on South Street, New York. With this intent they purchased the steamer "William Penn," and fitted her out as a pioneer. She was a small ship even in those days. Now, she would not be much too large for a quarter boat to be hoisted at the davits of the modern sea monsters. Still, she was an excellent sea-boat, although of only

613 tons, and having been built for the line between Philadelphia and Boston, her accommodations for twenty or thirty passengers were as comfortable and luxurious as those of the British steamers. Her first trip was to be made under the most favorable conditions of summer weather, and it was confidently expected that every berth would be speedily taken, and that her small space for cargo would at once be availed of. She was placed under my command, and in view of the demand for state-rooms, only a small cabin was reserved for myself, wife and child. She was advertised to sail in fifteen days from the 5th of May, not only in the New York papers, but likewise in those of Philadelphia, Baltimore and Boston. To our intense chagrin, day after day passed without a single application for freight or passage, until I suggested to Mr. Mc-

Cready that as his enterprise was likely to be a complete failure, he had better withdraw the advertisements, and sell the ship, or find some other use for her. But he was a man of determination, as was afterwards proved when he established the Old Dominion Line to Richmond and made of it a triumphant success. "No," he said, "we will not give it up. Take coal enough for your return voyage, and see what you can get in Marseilles to bring back to New York." This was done, and we started on the 20th of May without a single passenger or a pound of freight. The steamer was advertised in the Marseilles and Paris papers to take freight or passengers to New York, and there was not a solitary application for either. Forty-two years have since elapsed, and what a change! American sailing ships have entirely disappeared from the Mediterranean and practically from all salt water excepting that which washes our coasts. The Mediterranean trade has increased to immense proportions and is now carried on almost entirely by steam. There are four great lines of steamships of from four to eight thousand tons, and innumerable tramps carrying thousands of passengers and millions of tons of freight, and earning for their owners wealth enough to pay the interest of our national debt. Not a single one of them is under our flag, simply because Congress persists in maintaining restrictive navigation laws that forbid us to own ships unless they are built at home at exorbitant prices, which preclude competition with other nations who adopt a more liberal policy.

When we arrived at Marseilles the cholera was just commencing its work, and every other Mediterranean port placed vessels from that city in strict and long quarantine. There was consequently nothing for any of us to do, and nowhere for any of us to go, and I was determined not to return to New York as we had come out, in ballast. So we all lay perforce huddled up in the docks under a broiling sun. The cholera was first said to be confined to the barracks and hospitals. Every effort was made by the authorities for a time to keep secret the advent of this unwelcome visitor; but when the numerous funerals began to pass along the streets, when in the cafés and on the Exchange men fell down in the agony of its grasp, concealment became a vain endeavor. Then ceased the characteristic gaiety of the Frenchmen, and in its place came despondency and abject fear. Out of a city of 250,000 inhabitants 100,000 of

the survivors rushed to the country, those
who could afford to do so by means of
railroads and carriages, those who could
not, on foot, and thus they might be daily
seen hastening in crowds to encamp upon
the hills, where, under the fierce rays of
the sun and the noxious dews of night,
they died by thousands. In the city all
was gloom and despair. Whole streets
of shops were closed. Nature seemed to
participate in the misery of man. For
three months not a drop of rain fell from
the heavens. Daily the lurid sun rose in
the east to set at night in the burning
west scorching in his progress all vegeta-
tion, and drying up the streams or reduc-
ing them to pools of stagnant water.
The sympathy of man for his fellow-man
was blunted and his heart beat only in
fear for himself. Thus coward man
trembled, and woman alone was brave,

brave in the might of purity and of love. In the splendid mansion, in the wretched hovel, wherever disease and death were to be found, there too were to be seen those self-sacrificing Sisters of Charity ministering to the wants of the sick and giving the dying a foretaste of heaven in the companionship of angels upon earth. These are the genuine saints of the Catholic Church.

As the autumn advanced the disease abated, and the panic-stricken refugees returned to their homes. Confidence was at length restored, and an instantaneous change came over the city. One would have supposed that death had never entered into the world, and that life would never go out of it. From the depth of misery the whole population mounted to the pinnacle of mirth. This was French.

In the meantime the Crimean War was going on. Its progress is worthy the attention of those of us who were so impatient with what they considered the dilatory proceedings of our armies at the time of the secession. This war had been for months and even years anticipated by France and England. They both possessed large standing armies fully equipped and disciplined, and their combined fleets exceeded those of all the world in ships, guns and men. All these existed in a time of profound peace. Yet at the date of which we are speaking, how little, or rather how much of nothing, had been accomplished! As we pursue our narrative, let us note how much time was still to elapse before anything was done; and as we come to its close let us see if this tremendous armament effected anything, after all, worthy of its boasted efficiency.

We shall find that we who had been suddenly dragged into a strife which we deemed so unnatural as to be impossible, and were consequently totally unprepared for it, had nothing to be ashamed of in comparison.

When their preparations were at last completed, and their fleets were already off the shores of the enemy, war was finally declared by France and England in March, 1854. What had since been done? The great Baltic fleets, which were to return ballasted with the guns of Cronstadt, had twice performed an evolution similar to that recorded, when "The King of France with twice ten thousand men, marched up the hill and then marched down again," and nothing had been accomplished in the Black Sea excepting that the battle of the Alma, to which we shall presently refer, had just been fought.

It is well known that the ostensible cause of the difficulty between Russia and Turkey in the first instance was the pretended desire of the former to protect her co-religionists in the Turkish domains, and to secure to them equal rights with the other subjects of the Sultan which to all intents and purposes they already enjoyed. It was only a pretext to cover her ambitious designs. In the mirror of destiny she had long seen Turkey in her possession, and time has been the only question in the matter. She would undoubtedly, if entirely successful, have solved the problem at once; but she was unprepared for the emergency which was thrust upon her. Since the war, with capital loaned by her former foes, she has constructed lines of railroads by means of which, should they hereafter endeavor to thwart her schemes, she can concentrate an overwhelming force to oppose them.

The fleet which left the Bosphorus in the summer of 1854, was known to carry a force destined to attack some part of the Russian territory in the Black Sea. It was generally supposed to be directed upon Odessa. The movement was conducted with much secrecy and skill, but it failed in its anticipated results from want of thorough organization and from a deplorable ignorance of the country it was intended to subdue. After various feints of attack upon other points, the course was finally changed to the Crimea, where the fleet arrived before the Russians could oppose a sufficient force to prevent the landing of the troops. They made, however, a gallant resistance after the invaders had debarked. The whole of the small garrison of Sebastopol came out to meet them upon the heights of the Alma. There the first battle was fought. It was chronicled as the first great victory of the allies. On the other hand, the Russians justly regarded it as the first check upon them. It was reported in France, where we happened to be at the time, that Sebastopol itself had fallen, and for a week people believed it. There was the most boisterous rejoicing. In Marseilles the affair was dramatized with incredible dispatch. It was represented in the theatre before a delighted audience on the very night preceding the day on which was brought the contradictory intelligence. Then was exhibited another proof of the ups and downs of French character. As the monarch of the barnyard flaps his wings and crows on a bright sunny morning, so the jubilant Frenchman strutted the boulevards, swung his cap and cried

"*Vive la France! Vive la gloire!*" As the same proud bird after a storm of cold rain presses his pinions to his sides, utters his mournful caw and drags his drooping tail feathers in the mud, so the utterly confounded Frenchman, when the storm of disappointment overwhelmed him, vented his "*Sacres*," withdrew his forehead into the crown of his hat, dropped his jaw under his shirt collar, and tried to hide himself in his boots.

The Russians, after vainly opposing a superior force, had retired in good order to Sebastopol, and immediately commenced throwing up those entrenchments which for eleven months afterwards bade defiance to the most unparalleled energy of attack. The town was already impregnably fortified against all attempts from the sea, as the fleets shortly afterwards discovered on the occasion of their ineffectual bombardment.

The news of the battle of the Alma and its want of entire success created an intense excitement in France and England. It had been imagined that this expedition into the Black Sea would have been sufficient to disperse the Russian forces from its shores, but all at once the Western powers awoke to the seriousness of their mistake. The capture of Sebastopol, though of course exceedingly desirable, as the destruction of the Russian fleet would have ensued, was not of absolute importance. But it was now more than ever determined upon as a matter of pride. It could have been blockaded, and all the other operations of the war might have been carried on nearly as well by that means as by the final conquest of only a portion of the town. Thus, many thousands of lives might have been spared, but the pride of France and England was touched, and they were determined to enter Sebastopol, though obliged to wade through the blood of their own children.

CHAPTER II.

THE " William Penn" was the first transport under a foreign flag chartered by the French government. We left Marseilles on the first of November with a cargo of stores and ammunition and a detachment of troops for the Crimea. With pleasant weather, which is rare even in the Mediterranean at that season, we passed through the Straits of Bonifacio between Corsica and Sardinia, and then through the Straits of Messina, lighted by the fires of Stromboli and Etna. Thence steering across for the Morea, we rounded Cape Matapan and entered the blue Ægean Sea. Everywhere the landmarks of the past greeted our eyes. There were the lands and the waters of great deeds made infinitely greater by the poetry of history, for poetry is the history of Greece and Troy. As we look back upon them through such telescopes, truly the distance of time lends enchantment to the view, and the eye gains delight by viewing them with a lens which softens their rougher outlines. Mythology, the poetical religion of the ancients, is more worthy of study than the story of their everyday life. The one, though false, is full of charm; the other, though real, was too much like that which we now see around us. Homer and Virgil were the best historians of those early days. Homer borrowed wreaths from the skies to adorn the brows of such barbarians as Hector and Achilles. Virgil called from them a goddess to give birth to the filibustering Æneas, and chiselled his black inamorata into the form and features of an angel.

At dark on the evening of the 9th we passed between the Island of Tenedos and the plains of Troy. Afterwards repeatedly we saw them in broad daylight. Then a black rock and a barren shore were displayed to ruin the picture imagination had painted of besieging Greeks and beleaguered Trojans.

We were about entering the Dardanelles, the ancient Hellespont. It should not have been attempted in a foggy night, especially as the narrow and crooked Strait was unlighted. But our orders were imperative to follow the French gunboat which bore us company. The result of this temerity was that we both found ourselves snugly ashore before morning. We grounded on Nagara Point, the very spot where Leander landed when he swam the Hellespont, and where Leander had more occasion to be pleased in getting ashore. We were unable at the time to back off, but fortunately the ground was soft, and no damage was eventually done to either of the ships. It was, after all, perhaps a fortunate accident. Had not this detention occurred, we should in the ordinary course of the voyage have been off Balaklava in the destructive gale of the fourteenth of November.

It was the occasion of my first acquaintance with a nation from whose people I have since received much kindness, and at no time a greater proof of their generous disposition than in this instance. As soon as morning dawned and the ship was discovered from the town, the Pasha of the Dardanelles came off in person to offer his assistance, which was, of course, gratefully accepted. In less than an hour a fleet of boats was alongside discharging cargo to lighten the ship, the troops being provided for in the Turkish barracks on shore. All the men that could be advantageously employed were sent to expedite the removal of the cargo. The Pasha himself remained on board most of the time. His kind expressions of sympathy were really consoling, and when at last the steamer floated off, his satisfaction seemed equal to my own. Suleyman Pasha was a strict observer of the forms, and precepts too, of his religion. When the hour of prayer came he turned his face toward the tomb of the prophet, and prostrated himself in devotion upon the deck. At evening for a few moments work was suspended, while all the people bowed in prayer. Suleyman dined with us every day. Upon the principle of not making one's brother to offend, I had given directions to exclude wine from the table. Think, then, of my astonishment at a gentle hint from the Pasha as to champagne! It was, of course, immediately produced. Upon my remarking that it had not been offered before on account of regard to what I supposed to be his religious scruples, he replied with an air of perfect sincerity, "Wine was forbidden by the prophet; not champagne. Champagne did not exist in his day; how then could he have forbidden it? Marshallah! God is great," continued Suleyman, smoothing his beard and soothing his conscience. "Pass the bottle."

While the ship was reloading I visited him at his house, meeting with a most cordial reception, and was there permitted to see the Turkish gentleman in his harem. This word has been the subject of the grossest misapprehension. The harem means the home; and the home of the Turk, though different in many respects from ours, is equally sacred. The Turkish woman is by no means always the degraded creature that many have supposed her to be, but she is often well educated and seldom unable to read. She is a faithful wife (though frequently not the only wife), and it may seem astonishing to many women in other lands who cannot live peaceably with their husbands, having them all to themselves, that these women can be happy not only in their husband's society, but in that of each other. In a state of polygamy, woman is not so lightly esteemed by man, but man is held in higher estimation by woman. We have scarcely a right to reproach the Turks for practising a polygamy that is cumulative while the laxity of our divorce laws permits it in a consecutive form among ourselves.

After a detention of three days caused

by our mishap, we were reloaded and ready to proceed. It had been a period of incessant work day and night, such as we could not have accomplished with our own boats and crew in many days. When about to leave, Suleyman Pasha was on board. I asked him what was the amount of expense incurred, that I might pay it by a draft on Constantinople. Seizing my hand and placing it upon his heart, he replied, "God pays me, my brother." I shall never forget that Christian Mahomedan.

Issuing from the Dardanelles we entered upon the Sea of Marmora, a salt water lake about one hundred and twenty miles in length. Leaving soon after midnight, on the evening of the next day we were within a few miles of Constantinople, when the heavy gale came upon us which was still more violent in the Black

Sea, and was the cause of terrible destruction of life and property. We were obliged to haul off, as we were on the lee shore, and to hold our own were forced to carry all the steam that our boilers could bear. The night was one of great anxiety; but, as after all nights of affliction, joy came in the morning. The gale abated; the angry waves fell quietly again upon the bosom of the Marmora, over which the sun rose in his full blaze of living light and shone back again from the gilded domes and minarets of the queen city of the East. There she lay before us, exceeding all the splendor with which imagination had clothed her, decked with the jewelry of her first love, and her ravisher. The daughter and rival of Rome, her beauty, matured in Oriental luxury, soon eclipsed her mother's fading charms. Mistresses of the Western and Eastern empires in the days of their glory, now in the days of their decadence, both so low in the scale of nations. We rounded slowly the point where stands the old Seraglio, at whose name Christian hair has been wont to stand on end, passing so closely under its windows that had a faithless sultana been dropped at the moment we might have caught her upon our decks. The practice of making such useless disposition of women, however, is not in vogue in our days.

In the harbor it was a busy scene. Light caiques propelled by lusty oarsmen were dancing about on every side, interspersed with boats from foreign and Turkish men-o'-war and merchantmen, and as we ran up the Turkish flag and fired a salute, we received in all tongues cheers of welcome.

The first appearance of the American

flag in the fleet, although it floated from the peak of a transport steamer, was evidently hailed as an indication that our national sympathy was enlisted in the cause. At subsequent times, under a summers sky, the Golden Horn was found more enchanting; but the first impressions of Stamboul and Pera, as they towered above us on either side in marble columns, are the longest to endure. And yet at any season the whole charm of Constantinople is lost when once upon the shore. The wretched and filthy condition of the streets, especially in the Christian quarters, creates a feeling of intense disgust. Would you visit this farfamed city, remember the whited sepulchres. Observe it well on every side, but within look not. From the deck let your eye and imagination rove from minaret to minaret, and thence wander to the natural scenery which gives them their charm. The Bosphorus, the Golden Horn, and the Sea of Marmora, encircling the picturesque architecture of temples and kiosks, afford a perpetual scene for admiration and delight. Well do I remember one morning when the declination of the sun brought him at his rising directly over the hoary summits of the distant hills, and the sudden change from gray twilight to blazing day, as from thence he threw abroad his spreading beams on heaven and earth and sea, lighting such a picture of nature and art, till every feature was so lovely that it would have been marred by the contrast of any shade. But evening has a charm above that of the day. As it draws on every one quits his toil, if toil it can be called where there is such general indolence. The lazy Turk, the ever-joyous Greek, the sly Armenian, and even the grasping Jew, all seek for recreation then. Hundreds of caiques are seen shooting over the waters to places of resort upon the Bosphorus, the Islands of the Marmora, or the Sweet Waters which lie at the extremity of the Golden Horn.

As we afterwards lay at the navy yard, how often have we seen these happy parties returning. Nature painted a living picture; the moon threw shadows of tall cypresses and taper masts upon the silver mirror, its polished surface broken only by the silent dip of oars. The stillness of the hour was stiller as it seemed to be listening to the dream-like music of the lute and tambourine, while the veil of mist which nightly shrouds the waters hung like a thin gauze over the fairy-like turrets of the city.

Receiving renewed orders from the

agents of the French government, we proceeded up the Bosphorus and entered the Black Sea. After the battle of the Alma, when the allies had discovered that Sebastopol was not so easily to be captured as they had imagined, they made their preparations to invest it. For this purpose they took advantage of convenient harbors to land their munitions and troops. A nearly equilateral triangle may be supposed, having for its points Sebastopol, Balaklava and Kamiesh. The first was occupied by the Russians, the English took possession of the second, and the French of the third. The area of this triangle served during the war for the outposts of the Russians and the encampments of the allies, and the neighborhood on the inland side was the great battlefield on which all the subsequent actions were fought.

Balaklava is completely land-locked, having an exceedingly narrow and crooked entrance, which makes it when entered one of the best harbors in the world. But it is very small. This did not seem an objection to it at that time, for no idea was then entertained of the extensive use to which it would afterwards be applied. The English accordingly, with the consent of the French, appropriated it for their vessels. The disadvantage arising from this error was proved first in the terrible hurricane of November 14th, in which so many English transports, unable to find shelter in the inner harbor, were wrecked upon the rock-bound coast. At the same time the French loss was slight, their harbor being sufficient to retain all their ships. Subsequently I have seen twelve hundred sail of vessels safely moored within it. We were ordered to

Kamiesh, and arrived there after a passage of a day and a half, the distance being three hundred and fifty miles from Constantinople.

I have thus with digressions not a few, gone over the ground from Marseilles to the Crimea, and as the same passage was afterwards repeatedly made, the narrative of one may suffice for all. At the time of our arrival there prevailed the famine and distress which the survivors of the English army still hold in sad remembrance. There was absolute starvation in their camp, while at four or five miles' distance provisions were rotting upon the beach. Much has been said of the mismanagement of the British government and of the superiority of the French commissariat. There is a certain degree of truth in this, but the neglect was not so extreme as has generally been supposed.

The English made many mistakes. Their first and greatest arose from a misapprehension of the enemies they had to deal with—the Russians and the Russian climate. A summer's cruise was projected to capture the little town of Sebastopol and to return with the guns of its fortress at about the same time that those from Cronstadt were expected to arrive. But before they accomplished this part of the undertaking, the other part being indefinitely postponed, they were obliged to carry a great many more guns there. They supposed that a few miserable Tartars, the abject slaves of the Czar, would be eager to hail them as deliverers. But they caught Tartars that they did not expect. They found that patriotism was as ardent and self-sacrificing among the inhabitants of the Crimea as among those of any other lands that they had before endeavored to conquer. The lesson of Bunker Hill had been forgotten. No people should be despised who have their own soil to defend.

Added to this motive for resistance there was a determined spirit of religious enthusiasm to meet, for the Russians had been taught that the war was waged against their Church. "God, and your native land!" the battle-cry of Bozzaris, nerved likewise their arms for the defence of their inheritance.

The English were unfortunate in the selection of Balaklava for other reasons besides the smallness of its harbor. It was at a greater distance from their camp than was Kamiesh from the headquarters of the French, and the road to it was chiefly of clay. While therefore the French managed with difficulty to keep up communication with their port, that of the English was nearly cut off. Four miles was sometimes a day's journey for a man on foot. The road was packed with animals that had died in their tracks. Under such circumstances it was absolutely impossible to transport sufficient provisions for an army. While the French barely succeeded in doing it on account of a better road and a shorter distance, the English could not do it at all.

There was another reason for their greater suffering, which observation warrants me in believing important. A Frenchman can live upon what is starvation to an Englishman; he can adapt himself to short allowance as no other mortal can. But an Englishman remembers his roast beef and his beer, and if he cannot get them, he will growl and lie down and die. Three or four Frenchmen can live upon the rations of one

Englishman, and be more jolly upon their empty stomachs than he would be with a tight waistband. When everything else fails, they can live upon ragouts made of remembrances of the past and seasoned with hopes of good times to come.

Once after a toilsome tramp to the English headquarters, my purser and I entered the tent of an officer with whom we were acquainted. Woebegone he looked, as he gave us a grouty welcome. "Come in," said he; "sit down. I wish I had something to offer you, but I have not. Expected a dozen of porter and a pair of fowls up to-day. Couldn't have cooked the fowls if they had come. No coal. However, might have lived a day or two on the porter, but done out of that too. Infernally miserable, by Jove!" And so he was. He looked it all.

Feeling little inclined to accept the only hospitality he had to offer—that of a camp stool,—we pursued our way tediously to the French camp, where our gay friend, Lieut. Courtois, was quartered. Before reaching his tent we heard a snatch from an opera. With what *empressement* he rushed to embrace us, invited us to dine, insisted upon it, and sent for some of his comrades to meet his guests! His larder was scarcely better stocked than that of the Englishman, which had nothing in it. But roots were grubbed up and a fire was made, some rough boards were laid out, and a clean cloth spread upon them. On came the soup, hot, at any rate, if it was homœopathic. And in the other courses, which were numerous, beans, the material of the soup, were disguised in infinite variety with such skill that they served for fish,
4

roast, *entremets*, and dessert. I am sure that we had salad of something; perhaps it was an old green silk umbrella. A little red wine was eked out with water, upon which we all pretended to be excited as we drank the health of the Emperor. Beans again—as, alas! too often with us at home—served for coffee, and my jolly friends after dinner tramped along with us on the road for a mile, imagining we were all on the boulevards, and sharpened their remembrances of departed joys by addressing every one they met as Mademoiselle.

CHAPTER III.

WITH the imperfect geographical knowledge of the country, which has been noted, and with not the most remote idea of spending the winter there, the allies had entirely neglected preparations for it. The rainy season came upon them suddenly. Hence the deplorable condition which resulted from not having constructed roads over which to transport their provisions. Not having the happy faculty of adaptation inherent in the French, the English starved until a railroad was brought out from home. Then John Bull had enough to eat and he was contented. Without the bounding impetuosity of his ally he has a bull-dog courage when cornered, and he never loses it. He marches up to the cannon's mouth, and meets a death which has no fears for him equal to those of a hungry life.

The great battles of Balaklava and Inkerman had been fought, each chronicled in English history as victories, although the former was a decided triumph of the Russians. From the results of both, all parties were satisfied that the contest was not to be decided by pitched battles, but that it was to be a work of siege, and thenceforward with occasional skirmishes the science of attack and defence occupied their chief attention.

It had never been anticipated by the Russians that the south side of Sebastopol would be exposed to an enemy. It was already fortified to an extent that would prove impregnable from the sea, while the north side, to which they eventually retired, continued impregnable to the end of the war. It may therefore be truly said that the fortress of Sebastopol has never been taken. The fleet moored in the harbor was at first almost the only protection from any attack from the south, till the wonderful genius of Todleben threw up the earthworks of the Malakoff, the Redan and the outer forts while the allies were deliberating upon a plan of operations.

Had they landed first at Balaklava and Kamiesh, they might have taken the city with ease, but they could not have held it even then, as the north side commanded it. The Russians always would have been perfectly secure upon that side to which they eventually retired. Their efforts were now directed to the possible salvation of the city and the fleet. Sebastopol never could have been completely invested with less than half a million of men. Consequently roads were kept open at all times to bring them reinforcements and provisions. Their great difficulty was in getting these from a distance, and their principal loss of men was occasioned by fatigue upon the road in the winter season. Many more perished in this way than in the defence of the town.

Meanwhile the allies commenced the work of the trenches. It will be readily understood, especially by those who have had sad experiences in our Civil War, that it was impossible for a body of men without cover to march several miles towards a fortified city, dragging with them their siege train with which they expected to batter down its walls. It was necessary to travel in a ditch, and that not a straight one, which would have been exposed to a raking fire. These ditches or trenches were accordingly dug in a zig-zag manner, so that, nautically speaking, the besiegers could "work up at short tacks." The dirt was thrown up on the side next to the city, in order to afford additional cover, and the whole with the embankment was of sufficient depth to protect the troops who passed along. This trenchwork was the severest trial they were called upon to endure. Added to the inclemency of the season was the necessity of night work to prevent the enemy from taking accurate aim. Notwithstanding this, many bombs fell in the midst of the working parties, and the explosions were awfully fatal. Wherever heads were shown in the course of their work, they were exposed to a rain of bullets.

But all this was as nothing compared to the cold and wet which brought upon them fevers and cholera, enemies more to be dreaded than the Russians. Tedious and slow was their progress as they met with rocky soil, and as the heavy rains nearly drowned them in their holes. Still they worked on, continually expecting sorties which were almost nightly made. Anxiously they waited for the dawn which would give a little relief to the miserable survivors of the night, who could then drag their wearied, stiffened limbs to their tents. Even there their covering was little better than the open air, like their bed on the ground, chill and damp. No consolation was theirs that they were fighting for their country's sake; they were hired by their governments to fight for what they knew not, and to die with curses upon them in the cold embrace of the soil which they had invaded. It was only in the delirium of fever that happiness existed, when the spirit transported from the wretched body saw and tasted sumptuous fare, wandered in the green fields of boyhood, or reclined upon the luxurious couch of ease, was clasped in a mother's fond arms, or received again the long remembered kiss of love. Happy was he who did not awake from his dreams to feel once more the reality of woe!

It was no pleasure for us to visit the camps and trenches where sights of misery were so constantly present. Curiosity was soon satisfied, and we realized that glory bought at such prices was dearly bought indeed. The condition of the Turks was in some respects more pitiable than that of their allies. No one seemed to care for them; for their ignoble retreat at Balaklava they were heartily despised by their friends as well as by their enemies, and till they redeemed their character at Eupatoria, were treated with scorn and neglect. I have actually seen a mule and a Turk harnessed together to a cart, and a Frenchman riding upon it and whipping up the team!

Such was the condition of the armies before Sebastopol at the close of December, 1854. Afterwards the state of things became worse as the rigor of the season increased.

The troops subsisted mostly on "hard tack," and on every return from Constantinople we bought up all the fresh bread the bakers could supply, so that, although on the passage it became somewhat stale, it was eagerly sought for at any price we might choose to demand, and it is a satisfaction to remember that the price demanded was not exorbitant. On the contrary, it was a sufficient reward to be able to contribute to the relief of the poor fellows who were so sadly in need.

In this connection I cannot forbear to mention the delicacy of the French Intendant, which was carried to such an absurd extreme, that he refused to dine on board àt our abundant and comparatively luxurious table lest an unworthy motive should be attributed to him. I can truly say that in all my intercourse with the business officers of the government I never saw the least sign of bribery or corruption. I believe that nearly all the money disbursed by France, nominally for the expenses of the war, was actually expended for that purpose. I wish that the same could be said of my experience in the transport service of our Civil War, to prosecute which an enormous national debt was incurred—no small part of it for individual benefit.

The Frenchmen were determined in all cases to get value received for what they paid out, and with this end in view they kept us so busily at work that towards the close of that winter I was glad to get an order to proceed to Marseilles, where it was found necessary and convenient to make extensive repairs to boilers and machinery. These having been completed, we renewed our accustomed routine of the transport service, leaving Marseilles deeply laden with shells and other war materials in the hold, four hundred soldiers in the between-decks, and the upper deck encumbered fore and aft with horse stalls.

We had scarcely left the harbor when a furious mistral burst upon us. Down it came from the mountains, over the plains and into the Gulf of Lyons, where it had full play for its fury. The wind was dead aft, and we scudded before it with a full head of steam, to keep out of the way of the continually rising seas. These at length were too much for us, as they broke over the stern and either quarter flooding the decks and pouring down into the engine-room and the quarters of the troops, and finding their way into the hold. Some of the horse-stalls fetched away, and two of the horses were pitched through the skylight upon the heads of the cylinders, necessitating a stop of the engines until we could hoist them out and throw them overboard.

Doubtless those officers and soldiers afterwards marched up without fear or trembling to storm the ramparts of Sebastopol, but now they were utterly demoralized. They had been seasick, but were seasick no longer. Fright effectually took the place of the *mal de mer*.

It was indeed a critical situation. I dared not round the ship to, in order to bring her head to the wind, in which position she would have been comparatively safe, lest we should be swamped in the evolution. So we kept on running, the water gaining on us, until it got nearly even with the furnace fires, in spite of all that steam pumps and hand pumps could do. Recourse was then had to bailing with the deck buckets and with such as we could extemporize. One important effect of this process was that the panic was overcome, as the soldiers were forced into a bucket brigade and there was something to occupy their minds. The firemen steadily stuck to their duty, although they were knee-deep in water.

At last the fierceness of the gale moderated, the seas subsided, and we went on our way rejoicing, over smooth water and under sunny skies. I made a little speech to *les braves militaires*, thanking them for the service they had rendered to themselves and to the ship, and ordered a double allowance of cognac for them. Then they cheered me as a "*brave commandant*," and we were all happy because we had not been drowned.

When we reached Kamiesh we found that it had changed its appearance since we left it at the close of the winter. In place of the outdoor accommodations, a town had sprung up at the head of the Bay. It was like San Francisco in its youth. The story of gains to be derived from the wants of the armies had flown to all parts of Europe like those of the gold discoveries in California, and there was a general rush to secure a portion of the prize. The new and heterogeneous population was composed mostly of Greeks, Maltese, and Jews.

As the season advanced the roads had become more passable, and we improved the opportunity to ride about the plateau. There was only one carriage in Kamiesh, an old Russian drosky, a machine resembling a stage-coach with wheels and no body. I had hired this vehicle, to give my family a drive to Balaklava, a distance of eight miles, for the price of twenty-five dollars. Refreshments upon the road were also costly.

We passed the residence of Lord Raglan, an old farmhouse which his lordship would consider unfit for his horses at home, but it was a palace here surrounded by trees and vines. They were the only trees and vines that had been suffered to remain. Everything else of the kind had been cut down or rooted up for fuel. The climate does not differ much from that of New England, but the want of shade rendered the summer heat insupportable.

Balaklava, like Kamiesh, had wonderfully improved in appearance and comfort, but its crowded state soon made it a scene of greater suffering in summer than in winter. Surrounded by high hills and deprived of the circulation of air, the cholera made fearful havoc among the shipping and the inhabitants.

On our return to Kamiesh we deviated from the direct road to visit the Monastery of St. George. The religious character of this institution had preserved it and its grounds from the general devastation of the country around. Upon an eminence of six hundred feet overlooking the sea, whose waves were beating at the base of the cliff, it was at any time a picturesque object, but was now more attractive than ever as an oasis in the desert of war. Here some of the clergy had found a refuge, where they passed their time in devotions, doubtless offering fervent prayers for peace to descend upon their unhappy land. Their sad and careworn faces seemed to speak of sickened hearts and of hopes long deferred. We attended service in the Chapel, where the mournful cadence of their voices chanting in an unknown tongue, seemed to be a true interpretation of the language of their souls.

A lady of rank, from whom the invaders had wrested her property and whose mansion they had destroyed, whose husband was their prisoner in a distant land, had been afforded by the magnanimous foes who were waging this war of civilization, a place in the sanctuary to die. The only luxury she had enjoyed for months was that now upon her deathbed, in accents of broken French, she could tell her sorrows to one of her own sex, who came not from the land of her enemies, and thus could find consolation in mingled tears. Beautiful as was the place, the sad thoughts these scenes inspired, more sad than those of battlefields, made us not reluctant to leave it.

CHAPTER IV.

THE spring months were chiefly occupied in short and frequent trips between Kamiesh and Constantinople, and the business came to be almost as monotonous as that of a Long Island Sound steamboat. It was once, however, varied by a delightful trip to Yenikale and Kertch in the Sea of Azof, whither we were sent with supplies for the French and Turkish troops left there to garrison those towns recently captured from the Russians. We carried a small detachment of troops and a few officers whose society was most agreeable. It was an exquisite pleasure to see them feasting at the table. Their great desire was that some accident might happen to the machinery, so that they could have time to recuperate from their long enforced starvation.

I will here take occasion to say a word about our *cuisine*. The terms of our charter were in brief fifty thousand francs per month and our coal. Added to this was a tariff for board and lodging of the soldiers and officers. The allowance for the soldiers was one franc and sixty centimes per diem, and that for officers was graded according to their rank, from three francs upward to five francs, and six francs for a general, as if a general could eat more than a subaltern.

It is needless to tell those of my readers who have voyaged on passenger steamers that there was " no money " in this. On the contrary, it entailed considerable loss, but it was submitted to in consideration of the general profit derived from the whole contract. There was, moreover, a curious clause at the end of the charter party which was very verbose and minute in its specifications. It was this: "In case of disputes or misunderstandings between the government and the captain, the government shall be the sole arbiter." After all, that did not differ very much from the way in which our government proposed to arbitrate questions connected with the Monroe Doctrine.

On the first passage from Marseilles I essayed to be as liberal as possible in regard to the table. There was provided a good solid breakfast of tea and coffee, beefsteak, chicken, omelets, and buckwheat cakes; for dinner at two o'clock, we had soup, fish, roast meats, pies and puddings; and for supper, tea, and plenty of cold meat and other accessories. The soldiers were as amply fed as the crew, and it is sufficient to say that there was abundance fore and aft, and the receipts did not amount to one-half of the expenses. Strange as it may appear, there was universal discontent.

On our return from this first voyage to Marseilles I showed my agreement to a popular restaurateur, and he said, " I ask nothing more. I will take that contract and give bonds to satisfy the government." His proposition was accepted, and in order not to have two culinary régimes in progress at the same time, I paid off and discharged all my own crew excepting the chief officer and chief engineer, shipped a French one, and agreed to pay for myself, my family, the purser, and the two remaining officers the tariff rate for generals. In short, although we still flew the American flag at our peak, we became to all intents and purposes Frenchmen, so that we almost forgot our native tongue.

This arrangement worked admirably. There was coffee early in the morning, a *déjeûner à la fourchette* at noon, a dinner of an infinite variety of small dishes with abundance of *vin ordinaire* at six o'clock, and a cup of tea in the evening. The restaurateur made a little fortune out of his contract; the government was satisfied; the officers, soldiers and sailors and firemen were satisfied; the purser and I, relieved from all care, were better satisfied than any of them, and the only objection to it all came from the innate cravings of half a dozen American stomachs.

Our route along the coast of the Crimea, in an easterly direction, was picturesque and beautiful. The besom of war had not swept over the green fields and vineyards, for the civilizing allies had not there set their feet. There was not a point of land for the whole distance which we could not have approached within a stone's throw. Still, in order to keep out of the range of masked batteries and rifles, prudence dictated a proper degree of caution.

Around the Bosphorus everything is beautiful. Here beauty lay at the feet of sublimity. In the distance were rugged mountains and abrupt precipices seeming to frown upon the lovely landscape below, yet yielding it protection from the cold northern blasts and sending down streams in sparkling cascades to fertilize the valleys. Vineyards and orchards lined the coast, and in the background were immense fields of waving grain. There were hamlets above and towns below, churches and palaces here and there, everything denoting prosperity and happiness. The smile of the Almighty had not yet faded from this garden of His earth. What a change to us from a few hours past, and what a change was to be in a few hours to come!

Yenikale, the place of our destination, is a small seaport situated at the entrance of the Sea of Azof. While the cargo was discharging we rode across the country to Kertch, a distance of nine miles. We entered the city with a feeling of melancholy most oppressive. There but a few weeks before had been a thriving city, its harbor filled with peaceful traders, its magazines full of grain and merchandise, its 18,000 inhabitants thronging its streets or domesticated in their often splendid homes or kneeling at the altars of their magnificent churches, all in mankind's general pursuit of gain, pleasure and happiness.

Now the blackened stumps of mastheads showed where were the sunken hulls of the vessels. The grain was still smoking amidst the ruins of its storehouses, and this happy people had been driven like thieves from their own houses, all ransacked from garret to cellar, after a surrender in which protection of life and property had been most solemnly promised.

As we passed along the deserted streets, the empty buildings sent back the echo of our horses' hoofs, and desolation seemed to be in its tone. Even the churches were desecrated, and " There," pointing to a pictureless frame, a Russian priest, whose scared figure flitted about the ruin of his sanctuary, found only words to say,— " there was our Saviour, till an English sailor cut the canvas out." Seminaries of learning had been destroyed, and their libraries given to the flames. Their splendid museum, one of the richest in the world with treasures of antiquity, built upon the foundations of the palace of Mithridates, where cherished memorials of his time and even of antecedent ages had been piously collected, was ruthlessly sacked, not for the purpose of enriching temples of art elsewhere, as was done by Napoleon when he pillaged Italy, but for vandal pastime and insensate love of destruction, under the instigation of the same drunken frenzy that perpetrated murder and rape scarcely surpassed by the hell-hounds of Delhi and Cawnpore. What a comment upon the idea advanced by the Western powers that Russia required lessons in civilization from them!

The Turks who formed the garrison at Yenikale were very comfortably situated. They had driven in from the country a considerable number of cattle and sheep, so that they had plenty of beef and mutton, and to spare. As provisions of this kind were scarce at Kamiesh, we availed ourselves of the opportunity to obtain a supply. The purser and I accordingly repaired to the camp, and sought an interview with the Pasha in command, who received us with great courtesy, but he could speak neither English nor French and we had only about a half-dozen words of Turkish at command.

First, we made mutual salaams, and then sat down together on the grass; next I offered him and his officers some cigars. We smoked for a while in silence. Indeed, the whole occasion was one of silence. At last I drew a paper from my pocket and made a sketch of the steamer, which was tolerably exact and easily recognized; then I made one of a steer and another one of a sheep. They were distinguishable, for one had horns and the other had not. I showed it to the Pasha, and pointing to the representation of the steer, raised two fingers. He nodded an understanding assent. I then pointed to the supposed sheep and spread out the fingers of both hands twice. He realized that this meant twenty. Next I said in an inquiring tone, "*Evet?*" That means, "yes," and it is one of the six words that I knew. The Pasha nodded his approval and repeated "*Evet*" in an approving tone.

Thus much having been accomplished, I took a handful of sovereigns from my pocket and held them out to the Pasha in the palm of my hand. After some deliberation he gathered in eight of them, and then pressing my fingers on the ten or twelve that remained, indicated that I should put them back in my pocket. I did so, and pointed down to the harbor, whereupon he detailed some soldiers to round up the animals, and when they had got the requisite number together he ordered them to drive them down to the beach, from whence they were speedily put on board the ship. Only two words had passed between us, and they were all-sufficient. So that was the way in which I traded with a Turk. Had he been a Jew or a Yankee, many more words and sovereigns would have passed between us.

We took on board a number of invalids whom we were to transport to Gallipoli in the Dardanelles, and thence with a load of cattle, we again sailed for the Crimea. After clearing the Bosphorus we became enveloped in a thick fog for the whole passage across the Black Sea. It was not surprising, therefore, that we slightly overran the distance, and did not make a very good landfall. In consequence of this, serious disaster was narrowly avoided. Suddenly in the early morning the veil lifted and we found ourselves running directly into the harbor of Sebastopol and almost under the guns of Fort Constantine. Of course we were seen as plainly as we could see, and as we turned about in all haste to escape into the offing, shot after shot came booming after us, splashing the water all around, but fortunately there had not been time to get an accurate range before the fog shut down again. Never was a fog more gratefully welcomed. The Russians naturally supposed that we were making the best possible time towards Kamiesh, and so they banged away in that direction with the hope that a chance shot might take effect; but all this while we were steering due west as fast as our screw could revolve, and it was not until we were fairly out of gun-shot that we turned to the south, and then, after a sufficient detour, headed for the port of our destination.

The roar of artillery and the crack of rifles day and night had long since become so familiar that we came to regard them as part of our daily life, and as we were at a safe distance they did not disturb our sleep; but at daylight on the morning of the eighteenth of June we became conscious that there was something unusual in the air, as suddenly hell itself seemed to have broken loose. No one had dreamed of the preconcerted and simultaneous attack of the allies on the defences of Sebastopol, for we had supposed, as the beseigers themselves to their sorrow discovered on that disastrous day, that the trenches had not been sufficiently advanced for the assault.

Nevertheless, the attempt was now made,

and the battle was waged with varying success from early dawn until the darkness of night closed down upon the horrible scene of slaughter. There was no cavalry charge like that of Balaklava with artillery on only one side, but it was artillery on both sides now. When it was all over, the unsuccessful invaders were fifteen thousand less in number than when it began. At one part of the day this Quixotic charge was nearly successful, not a few of the French troops having succeeded in scaling the earth-works of the Malakoff.

All was consternation ashore and afloat at Kamiesh and at Balaklava, and every transport received orders to go to sea at a moment's warning. All day long bombs were whistling and bursting in every direction. A blaze of fire illuminated the sky from the horizon to the zenith, and terrific explosions causing the ships in the harbor to tremble to their keels, while

"Earth shook; red meteors flashed across the sky,
And conscious Nature shuddered at the cry."

We climbed to the mast-heads, and some of us went up to a little knoll two or three miles from the harbor to get a better view of the fight. But little more was to be seen excepting when, through the smoke "far flashed the red artillery;" and as stray shots occasionally ploughed up the ground around us, we did not remain long upon the hill.

The allies were finally repulsed, and before morning dawned, the town of Kamiesh was filled with the wounded. Had it not been for them there would have probably been a rush of everybody and everything on shore for the ships that would perhaps have tried to get to sea, for it was the general impression that the Russians would follow up their advantage, and come out in force to drive away their demoralized enemies.

As reports had come in from the battlefield during the day, not only the officials but the camp followers and merchants were most seriously alarmed. The latter picked up their belongings, and piteously begged for leave to bring them on board the ships, and it was not until the next day indicated that we should not be molested, that confidence returned and people resumed their usual vocations.

Fortunately for them, the besieged had suffered nearly as much as the besiegers and they were content with repulsing their assailants instead of following up the advantage they had gained. If they had been able to improve it we should have been at their mercy. There were thirteen hundred sailing vessels in the harbor of Kamiesh alone, and there would have been such a jam that we could not have gotten out. They might have set on fire and destroyed the whole fleet.

Such a contingency had often occurred to us, and there was a constant fear that among the Greeks who formed a part of the crews, there might have been some Russian spies who could on any night simultaneously have set a number of ships on fire to windward, and caused the unavoidable destruction of them all. With this in mind, I always selected a berth as near as possible to the mouth of the harbor and kept the fires constantly banked. It was strange indeed that this means of doing more injury to their enemies than could have been caused by sorties or battles was not improved by the Russians.

There was no time lost in the morning. Every steamer and sailing ship that could be utilized was ordered to make preparations to receive and carry away all the wounded that were not actually dying, to the hospitals below, and some of those who could bear the transportation to Marseilles. Hasty preparations were accordingly made by covering the lower decks with straw for human bedding as we bedded down the horses and cattle. Then the steamers took the sailing vessels in tow, and we all proceeded down the Black Sea, our destination being Marseilles.

From thence we were sent to Algeria to take a regiment of Zouaves to the Crimea. Owing to the necessity for some correspondence with France—which for want of telegraphic communication required a week for a reply—we had that time at disposal for a journey of a hundred miles in the interior to visit Constantine, the ancient capital of Jugurtha. It had been for many years a stronghold of the Arabs, and was wrested from them by the French after a prolonged siege, in which the garrison was starved out, the assault of the perpendicular cliffs on which the citadel was built being out of the question. The account of their heroic resistance, until famine compelled surrender, is historical, like that of the siege of Saragossa, and like that it will live for all time to come, and stir the hearts of patriots everywhere who are willing to sacrifice their lives in the sacred cause of their country.

CHAPTER V.

THERE was no railroad then to Constantine, and we travelled slowly by diligence, our road lighted at intervals by bonfires as a protection against the wild beasts that infested this region. Returning to our port of Philipville, we took the Zouaves on board and were ready for sea. As an instance of the unvarying attention and politeness of the French officers everywhere with whom we came in contact, I must record my obligations to the general in command, who invited us to dine, and then, taking me out to his stable, presented me with a beautiful Arab stallion. The docile creature became so accustomed to getting to and from the ship in a small boat, that I had the pleasure of horseback exercise in every port. When the steamer was sold at the close of the war, he was shipped in a return sailing transport to New York, and carried me many a mile in our own country until he was superannuated.

The allies sustained their heaviest losses in the summer months of 1855. They came more from disease than from battle. We perused with astonishment the accounts of what was transpiring around us, as they reached us in the French and English newspapers. "The sanitary condition of the army is excellent," was the stereotyped despatch to the London *Times* from Lord Raglan until he, himself, died with the cholera, and the same message was regularly sent in regard to the navy by Admiral Boxer, till he, too, was taken off by the same dread disease.

There was more of truth in the admiral's report than that of the general, for there was comparatively little sickness afloat, as the sailors were subjected to no exposure or hardship, and were better fed and cared for than the soldiers. But the messages of Lord Raglan and General Pelissier had their effect in deceiving their countrymen at home and encouraging perseverance in the war, while everybody on the ground knew they were stupendous falsehoods.

We transported some of the eighteen hundred survivors who were originally in the camp at Maslak, after it had been repeatedly announced that but a few cases of cholera had occurred there. In Eupatoria the garrison of thirteen thousand had been reduced to six thousand without a battle.

Among our passengers were frequently surgeons of the army and officers of high rank. They agreed in fixing as the lowest estimate the loss of the allies for that summer at thirty thousand men. Sickness was prevalent, too, among the civilians and aboard the ships. Our surgeon, to whom we owed a debt of gratitude for his sanitary precautions which kept us all in good health, was constantly occupied while we were in port. One day I said to him as he returned to the ship with a pocketful of napoleons and five-franc pieces, " Doctor, you get rid of more medicine here in two hours than you have dispensed on board the ship since you joined us." He replied, " Ah, well, you pay me by the month."

The secret of our immunity was that we never drank any water that had not been filtered elsewhere or distilled on board. In the naval fleet the water was never brought on board from the shore, but was always distilled. On land this precaution was perforce not taken. Still, something might have been done to prevent the soldiers from drinking the water of stagnant pools and streams polluted with the carcasses of dead animals that had been dumped into them to save the trouble of burial. It really seemed as if the allies were not content with being killed in their engagements with the Russians, but were determined to add to battle, and murder, the sudden death they brought upon themselves.

The men wounded in the various battles and skirmishes, as well as fever and cholera patients, were cared for as far as possible in temporary hospitals under canvas, for there were no buildings left standing when it was known by the Russians that the allies would occupy the territory around Sebastopol. The Moscow policy was adopted again.

So soon as the patients became convalescent or partly so, they were shipped to Scutari, where there was plenty of room for them and a better chance for their recovery. A large fleet of steamers was constantly employed in this transportation. On the return we were accustomed to bring recruits, horses, stores and ammunition. The lower deck, with the exception of the cabin reserved for officers, was fitted up as a permanent stable. When carrying cattle or troops, the bars between the stalls were removed, making room for four hundred cattle, two thousand sheep, seven hundred soldiers, or two hundred and fifty sick and wounded. The crowded condition of the little steamer, measuring only six hundred and thirteen tons, including the machinery, may be imagined. The cattle, however, were of a very small breed, and, being furnished by contractors with regard to number and not to weight, they were so thin that they could be easily stowed away, and so light that they were always hoisted in and out by the horns.

In our civil war, although there was an enormous amount of bribery, corruption, and stealing that was unknown in the French commissariat and intendance, there was seldom such overcrowding as this. An inferior class of transports was, however, employed, rotten old hulks, North River barges fitted with teakettle power, being accepted by our government officials —for a consideration. We were then, as we still are, prohibited from the purchase of substantial iron steamers from abroad, and such rattle-traps as these were necessarily employed for the emolument of their owners, who considered protection of home industry of this kind to be good policy. The coast from Maine to Florida was lined with these coffins of our soldiers, whose only satisfaction was, before they were drowned, that they were not packed as were these Frenchmen, like sardines in a box.

Upon arrival at Kamiesh, with any of these supplies from Marseilles or Constantinople, frequently scarcely an hour was allowed to cleanse the Augean stables. As the last package, man, beast or ammunition, went over the side, the hose was led to play on the decks, and whitewash was laid on the ceiling. The decks were then swabbed and clean straw was strewed upon them, whereon were placed the sick and wounded.

The unpleasant nature of this occupation may be readily conceived, and I will not shock sensibility by minute description of the objects of misery that came under our charge. Turned out from the camp hospitals where many of them might have survived, sometimes in a critical stage of fever or cholera, they were brought at early morning in ambulances or on mules, one slung on each side of the animal, and arrived at about eight or nine o'clock at the beach. There I have seen hundreds of them lying in the hot sun for hours, the steamers, or the scows in which they were to be floated off not being ready to receive them. There they groaned, and cursed, and prayed— prayed for death. Many died upon the beach and upon the short passage to the ship, and some died as they were being carried up the ladders. As we steamed away at our fullest speed, many a poor fellow found his grave in the Black Sea. The Euxine is its rightful name in geography and history, but now it came to deserve the name by which it is more often called.

Familiarity with misery and death tends to make the hearts of men callous, and dries up the fountains of sympathetic tears. One day as I was taking my rounds in the between-decks, I came to a poor man in the last agonies of cholera. He was powerless to help himself, and his glassy eyes showed that he was beyond the reach of hope. Seated near him was another not severely wounded soldier, employed in mending his clothes. I said to him, " Why don't you try to do something for that poor fellow, and at least brush the flies from his face ? " " That's not my affair," he replied; " I did not come from the same hospital, and besides he belongs to an infantry regiment." "What is all that row about?" I asked a chief officer on another occasion. "It comes from some of the soldiers," he answered, "because we had to disturb their game of cards when hauling up a couple of dead men from the fore hatch."

But let us turn to the only humanizing feature of this sad experience—the never-failing sympathy and tenderness of those blessed Sisters of Charity. As soon as we anchored off Scutari, by day or by night, in summer or in winter, in sunshine or in storm, they were alongside the ship. At sight of them, the ferocious soldiers for the time changed their natures. When they descended among the sick, whose lips were almost sealed in death, grateful eyes spoke in clearer tones than words could express. They brought with them little delicacies to tempt the appetite, and ointments and dressings for the mangled limbs of the wounded. There they sat down upon the filthy straw among them, and when earthly succor was of no more avail, they soothed their dying moments by telling them of

> "A sovereign balm for all their woes,
> A cordial for their fears."

Florence Nightingale has nobly won a renown that will endure for ages, and this part of her reward she has upon earth. St. Arnaud, Raglan, Canrobert, Pelissier, Omar Pasha, Gortchakoff, and other heroes of the war have written their names in blood upon the scroll of history. The name of no one of these Sisters of Charity has been sounded by the trumpet of fame. Earth has never rewarded them, for they sought not wealth or applause, but their names have been written on the records of heaven, in tears of gratitude and holy love.

The main defences of Sebastopol, after a persistent siege of nearly a year, were at length captured on the 8th of September, 1855. The town, a wreck of brick and mortar, that had been riddled for so many months by a storm of iron, was evacuated by its remaining inhabitants. The old wooden fleet, comprising but few vessels fit for modern warfare, was scuttled and sunk in the harbor. In one night the Russian garrison, after thus disposing of the fleet, blew up the southern forts, crossed and burned the bridge, and retired unmolested to their northern Gibraltar, which commanded the ground that they had previously occupied, thus performing the most masterly evolution of this eventful war. Everything of value that was left to their enemies were the splendid docks whose position sheltered them from the Russian guns. Actuated by the same vandal spirit which led them to destroy the treasures of antiquity of Kertch, they proceeded systematically with the destruction of these works unequalled by any others at that date.

A few days afterwards we visited the captured city, having hired the same old drosky on which we made the excursion to Balaklava months before. It was nearly the only four-wheeled vehicle that could be obtained, and its owner derived a large income from its profitable employment, at the rate of a dollar per mile. My wife could sit upon it with difficulty, but it was necessary to pass lashings over the young lady of six, whose curiosity, like that of her mother, was bombproof. First we proceeded over a tolerably good road through the French headquarters, stopping for a moment to pay our respects to General Pelissier at his little ten-foot shanty, and then went on to the English camp, where we were politely received and furnished with a pass to enter Sebastopol. It was necessary to be provided with this, as a general admission was forbidden, it having been found that large crowds frequently drew a heavy fire from the north side, whereas, under this regulation, the risk was diminished.

The road, which, after leaving the French camp, had gradually been growing worse and worse, now became villainous as we bounded over it on this cart-frame without springs or cushions. For the last two miles the ground was literally covered with balls and fragments of shells that had been fired from the Malakoff and Redan. We passed several regimental cemeteries of the English. That of the 117th was neatly fenced and kept in order like a garden, presenting a pleasing contrast to the general inhuman disposition of the dead.

Being now on the Woronzoff road, we passed the Mamelon Vert. This fort had been in the possession of the allies for a long time, and under its cover the final successful rush was made, when the English were exposed to such a storm of shot as had seldom before been faced by an army, and which nothing but emulation could have enabled them to encounter. Standing there now it was difficult to imagine the possibility of its accomplishment, even if the thousands of dead who had been thrown into the ravine had already been there to lessen its depth. We first entered the Redan, and there, as afterwards at the Malakoff, all preconceived notions were dissipated. Instead of granite walls of masonry, there were barricades of sand-bags, more formidable and more easily repaired than fortifications of stone. From thence we looked down upon the city, which before had been seen but indistinctly. Now the whole town was exposed to view, and a melancholy view it was indeed. Scarcely a house had been untouched, and whole blocks and squares had been completely demolished. The mast-heads of the ships in the harbor were above water, and the pride of the Russian navy, "The Twelve Apostles," could be seen almost down to her deck. Forts Constantine and Catherine, were blazing away occasionally, principally upon that part of the town where the French were throwing up breastworks against it. We descended to the city merely that we might say that we had been in Sebastopol, and walked about what Gortchakoff so aptly termed its " bloody ruins." But we soon saw enough of its desolation, and were willing to leave this charnel-house, whose horrid odors had more effect in driving us away than the booming of the guns.

The estimate of plunder found in the city has been much exaggerated, the inhabitants having long before removed their money and valuables to places of safety in the country. The prey that remained was distributed in a ratio of two-thirds to the French and one-third to the English, each of whom made the Sardinians a small allowance. The Turks got nothing, it being supposed that they owed the whole of their share in gratitude!

Ascending a quarter of a mile, we stood upon the Malakoff, the key of Sebastopol. From its summit was the most comprehensive view, and the whole field of operations could be taken in at a glance. The tower of the Malakoff, of which so much has been said, was nothing but a small stone battlement, whose foundation only remained. The earthworks were like those of the Redan, excepting that they consisted of baskets of dirt and of rigging of dismantled ships, instead of bags of sand. The position far exceeded that of the Redan in size, strength and ability for desperate resistance. In both forts, as well as everywhere else in the vicinity, the ground had been ploughed up by shells, which must have cost the lives of thousands of the brave defenders.

From this height the labor of months and the result of the final conflict could be seen at a glance. Beneath lay the ruined city;

beyond, the harbor dotted with the mastheads of sunken ships ; further still, the bristling Russian batteries terraced above each other, and vomiting fire and shot upon the enemy, tantalized by the sight of an unavailable prize. Turning around and looking beneath we could see the long zigzag lines of attack, those of the French reaching to the base of the Malakoff. Thence the nimble Zouaves, who decided the fate of the day, sprang at the signal and scaled the parapets with a bound.

At the right and facing the Redan were the English works uncompleted in their length. By Pelissier's order, the English were obliged to storm the Redan under a disadvantage not shared by the French; for they were forced to run down a hill into the ravine, and thence to attempt an ascent which proved to be impossible. Nearly all were mowed down by the Russian guns and fell into this valley of the shadow of death, which became a vale of mortality made almost level with the bodies of the slain. The English were compelled to retreat. But the Redan was evacuated in the night, and they entered it unmolested in the morning.

The conflict was yet too recent for the dust of men and the dust of earth to be mingled together. Mangled and unburied corpses were still seen around, and the air was impregnated with this vast human sacrifice.

The brave soldiers who perished in the attack belong now to a legion of honor. The altar of patriotism is the monument of the defenders, and a halo of glory surrounds their memory—a memory forever enshrined in the heart of Russia, of the gallant band who withstood that year's long, fiery rain, not for honor, but for country and for home.

By a tacit understanding, the dinner hour had been respected during the siege, and both parties were allowed to dine quietly, and after a suitable allowance of time for pipes and cigars, fighting was resumed. It was therefore justly considered an affront by the Russians when this conventional truce was broken by the other side, and the French commenced the scaling of the Malakoff, just as they were sitting down at their noonday meal.

But now the practice had been resumed, and everything was quiet, till about two o'clock in the afternoon, when the Russians could be seen bestirring themselves across the bay. Forts Constantine and Catherine were becoming more energetic, and a little battery across the harbor began to exercise its mortars in our direction. We accordingly executed a speedy retreat across the ravine below the Redan where our cart was in waiting. Just as we were driving away, a shell burst in the centre of the Malakoff and another over the path on which we descended.

Here is an extract from a letter written on the next day to a Boston newspaper:

"To own the truth, however incumbent it was upon me, as your correspondent, to enter Sebastopol, I felt that I had incurred a risk for others who were of vastly more importance to me than are the readers of the *Journal*. But 'all's well that ends well,' and I do not regret it now. Female curiosity has been satisfied. What American woman would depart from the neighborhood of such a scene without investigating it, regardless of a little danger, and years hence (God bless her! may it be many of them!) my little daughter may tell her children of the ever memorable siege of Sebastopol, and of that lovely autumn day when she stood upon the Malakoff and clapped her hands with delight as the balls came whizzing over her head."

CHAPTER VI.

OUR contract with the French government had now nearly expired, and although it might have been renewed, it was not advisable. As has been already intimated, the French, while strictly honorable in all their dealings, were hard task-masters, and were always on the alert to get the full worth of their money. There was a clause in their charter party to the effect that any delay on our part caused by accident to the ship or machinery should incur a reduction of pay corresponding with the time lost thereby. If we shut down steam for an hour or two, even if we made the same speed under canvas, while prosecuting repairs, it was sure to be reported by some one of the passengers. But it was "nominated in the bond," and we had no right to complain of it.

Nevertheless, the conditions were so onerous that, as the Turkish government offered the same rates, I concluded to become a Mussulman for the time being. In their service we had, on the whole, an exceedingly easy time. The French idea of putting off nothing for the morrow that could be done to-day was exactly reversed. Anything that should be done to-day was postponed till to-morrow excepting in case of dire necessity.

Having made the agreement with the Minister of War, I drew up a charter party similar to the one we had with the French, taking care, however, to omit the provision that in all disputes the government was to be the sole arbiter, and presented it to the Minister for his signature. He cast a half-awake look at it and asked, "What is that?" "The charter party, your Excellency," I replied. "A charter party? What is a charter party?" "Why, your Excellency, it is our agreement." "Our agreement!" he repeated after me. "Well, have we not agreed to pay you what you had from the French, —£2,000 per month and your coal?" "Precisely so," I answered. "And this is it." He took the paper, scanned it over, and then returned it to me saying, that there appeared to be a great many words used to express a very simple matter, and that there was no use for any writing, for all that I had to do was to come at the end of the month and get my money. Thereupon I told him that for my own part I needed no paper, as I was fully satisfied with his word, but that the other owners of the ship at home would object to my doing business in that way. "Ah, well," he replied, "if you must have a paper, make it short as possible. Sit down and write this: 'The Ottoman Government charters the William Penn at £2,000 a month, furnishing the coal and paying for passengers' food the same as heretofore."

I wrote that down accordingly, and having signed it, with a yawn he returned to his pipe and his coffee. The money was as punctually paid as if this simple charter party had covered a ream of paper, and although we went when we were told to go and stayed when we were not told to go, I honestly think that there was a great deal of pay for a very little work. Our trips were generally from Constantinople to Varna or Eupatoria, that is, when we did anything but lay at the dock.

On arrival it was my duty to report to Mustapha at the Arsenal. Always when admitted to his presence I found him cross-legged on the divan in exactly the same spot and position he occupied when I had last taken leave. He must have moved in order to go to bed at night, but it did not seem as if he needed to have done so, for he appeared to be asleep most of the time.

I made my habitual salaam, which he acknowledged with a slight nod, and then made a motion with his hand that I was to sit down, which I did, not after his fashion, but after my own. A sort of grunt brought a servant, and some kind of a signal, without the needless use of words, told him that he was to bring coffee and chibooks, both of which, particularly the coffee, I detested. Coffee prepared in Turkish style is an abomination of fine grounds stirred up with hot water strained through the teeth before it can be swallowed, and there is an unpleasant bitterness in the taste of their tobacco. Nevertheless, it would have been a breach of etiquette to decline the offered refreshments.

Silently we sat and sipped and smoked for perhaps ten minutes until the Pasha broke the dream-like stillness by asking, " When did you arrive ? " " This morning at eight o'clock, your Excellency." "I will send your coal to-morrow." That was all that there was to be said, and it was the end of the interview. The coal did not come on the morrow, but it came in little driblets towards the end of the week. Meantime the pay was going on, and I rather liked this change from the energetic practice of the French.

Once we were sent up to Eupatoria in the dead of winter with a cargo of stores. When we arrived, it was blowing a gale on a lee shore, and several vessels were anchored in the outer roads, rolling and pitching in the big seas that were tumbling on to the beach. We anchored ahead of a sailing ship, giving her, as I supposed, a sufficient berth. But instead of riding with two anchors with ninety fathoms of chain to each, she was riding with one hundred and eighty fathoms out at a single anchor in eight fathoms of water.

Suddenly in the night there was a fearful crash under our stern. In rising and falling on the seas, the propeller had struck the chain of the ship astern of us and was shivered at the hub, leaving the shaft bare! This was indeed a most unfortunate accident, for although no such contingency was provided for in the concise agreement drawn up by the Minister of War, I felt that I was in honor bound to claim no pay while off duty till another propeller could be substituted.

"This is a bad business, Mr. Sears," I said to my chief officer. Mr. Sears was a genuine Cape Cod Yankee, and I was greatly attracted to him for his sterling good qualities, and his characteristic humor was always enlivening. His experience had heretofore been entirely in sailing vessels, and he had a very poor opinion of " bilers and fireplaces " in the hold, and was always expecting a fire. But nothing ever disturbed the equilibrium of his philosophy.

Once, when in the French service, as we were crossing the Black Sea in a heavy gale, a fire broke out in some cotton waste in the engine-room. As I jumped below to see that the hose was led on, I shouted to Sears to keep the ship off before the wind, to lessen the draught.

A French General who happened to be on board, who would not have winked before the guns of Sebastopol, was, like many of the soldiers, paralyzed with fear. He rushed up to Sears, who was standing by the man at the wheel, exclaiming, "Oh, Monsieur Se—ars, ze ship vill burn, vill burn, vill burn!"

"Like enough," he replied, interjecting an order ("steady as you go"). "I've been cal'ating on that for some time. What can you expect when there is so much fire around? Mebbe we'll put it out, and mebbe we won't. You'd better get them sojers of yourn for'ard. I want to have the davit tackle falls ready for runnin'. Take it easy, Gineral, you can't do nothing but keep out of the way.

Whatever is fated will come to pass; that's sartain."

When we were shut up with all the other vessels in the port of Marseilles at the time of the fearful cholera visitation in the summer of 1854, and the fleet was abandoned to the care of ship-keepers, I offered to take him with us into the country, but he bluntly refused to go.

"I can look out for the ship better than any ship-keeper," he said. "If it is fated for me to catch the cholera, in course I shall catch it, and if it ain't, I shan't. No, sir, I am going to stay aboard, and get my grub ashore, if there is anything fit to eat. That's the worst of it, for these darned French dishes may give me the cholera after all; but that depends on how it is fated."

Sears was very reticent about matters pertaining to his home circle, and we had been away six months before any letter came to him. At last one day in the Consul's office I found one addressed to "Snow Y. Sears, First-mate of Steamer William Penn," having upon it the postmark of Hyannis. On handing it to him he put it into his pocket.

"Why, Mr. Sears," I said, "aren't you going to read your letter you have been waiting for so long?" "I haven't been waiting for it," he replied, "it's come of itself. I was going to keep it till after dinner, but I suppose I might as well read it now."

With that, he slowly opened it, glanced at the signature to see from whom it came, and then read it with unmoved features till he came to the close, when a smile stole over his countenance.

"Well, what's the news from home?" I asked. "Nothin' very particular," he answered. "Well, there is, though. A man in Hyannis has run off with a woman." "That's a rather common thing," I said. "Yes, but he was a married man." "That makes it worse." "But the woman was married too," he continued. "That's about as bad as it could be," I remarked. "No, it ain't," he replied. "The d——d rascal owed me two hundred dollars; but we're even now!"

"Why?" I inquired. "How does his running away pay his debt to you?"

"Well, sir," answered Sears, "when a man is bothered with one woman, it's generally bad enough, but when he's lumbered up with two, he is to be pitied more than two hundred dollars' worth, and I shan't foller him up any more."

The conclusion we arrived at after this was either that Mr. Sears was a bachelor, or that he would prefer to be one. He maintained his confidence in fatalism to the end. After his return to New York, when the yellow fever was raging in Havana, he was offered a command of a bark in that trade, a position that no one seemed to covet. But he accepted it at once. When some of his friends endeavored to dissuade him, he simply said, "If it is fated for me to catch the yellow fever, I shall catch it, and if it is fated the other way, I shan't." Unfortunately, this time fate was against him; he had the fever and died.

Dear, good, faithful, honest old soul, though not much of a Presbyterian, you believed in one article of their catechism, and you were predestined to receive your reward!

While I was in despair at the loss of the propeller Mr. Sears took this consolation to himself, "Well, we've got to be a sailing vessel now, anyway, and I begin to feel to home." Then after a little reflection, he added suddenly, "Captain, that propeller ain't gone—leastways it ain't gone yet."

"What do you mean?" I said. "It's very much gone, and gone altogether." "No, it ain't—yet," he replied, "and it won't be gone till them Turks find out it is gone, and then it'll be time enough for us to lose it. We've got to discharge this cargo, and the way things go among these fellers that'll take a week, and till then the propeller is just as safe as if it was on the shaft; and when we've got the cargo out, who knows what may turn up? Whatever will be, will be, and there's no use bothering about the futur' now. The best thing we can do is to turn in and get some sleep. It won't come off again to-night, anyway, and if the wind holds this way till morning we can get into the harbor easily enough without any propeller."

The wind did hold, and the gale abated, so that at daylight we hove up our anchors, made a little fire for the sake of appearances, hoisted the jib and sailed into port, anchoring among the rest of the fleet. As we brought up, Sears rubbed his hands and quietly remarked, " The propeller ain't gone yet."

The sentinels were pacing their rounds, but the camp was not yet awake. Fortunately for the invaders, the Russians had not had time to destroy the town in accordance with their usual practice, so that the quarters of the troops were more comfortable than they would have been in tented fields at this inclement season of the year, when, as on the day of our arrival, the mercury stood at zero, and the streets were blocked with snow. With what we had brought them, the garrison had a good supply of food, but scarcely enough fuel to cook it, and none whatever wherewith to keep themselves warm.

I made inquiries for the Pasha in command, and was directed to a house occupied by him. Through the interpreter I asked the guard in what room he was to be found, and he pointed out the door to me. On entering, I saw, literally, a pile of bodies, a dozen or more heaped up together and all asleep. They were awakened by the noise we made, and as they uncoiled themselves, the Pasha was discovered at the bottom of the heap, where he had kept himself warm by having men instead of blankets piled over him.

When he learned that a steamer had come to him with provisions, he soon got over his resentment at having been so rudely awakened, and when I expressed my sympathy and offered to send ashore a few tons of coal to warm up his house, he blessed me in the name of the Prophet and hugged me in his arms. From that moment he was our friend, and I verily believe that had the loss of the propeller come to his knowledge he would have carefully ignored it.

But that propeller was not yet gone. It took nearly a week to discharge the cargo in small boats, and in stormy weather, and truth compels me to say that we fell naturally into the Turkish habit of doing nothing to-day that could be done to-morrow.

At last what I supposed would be the inevitable day was drawing near when we should be ordered to return to Constantinople with invalids. But to my great relief the Pasha informed me that they had on hand a large amount of barley that had been captured from the Russians, and that he wished us to load with that instead of carrying passengers.

When I communicated this pleasing intelligence to Mr. Sears, I said that there might be a question as to its being fair to take that barley on board knowing that we could not carry it away under steam.

" Well," he replied, " barley ain't a perishable article, like a sick sojer, and if it should take a little longer to get it down to Constantinople, no harm will be done. It will be a week at any rate before we can get it in, and that time will be saved anyway. Then, like enough, we'll have a slant of wind to get out of the harbor, and we can lose the propeller going down the Black Sea."

This consideration of the subject seemed to be reasonable, and its adoption under the circumstances justifiable, as at the worst the minister of war would probably only deduct from our pay the difference of time occupied in sailing and steaming. So we commenced taking in the barley, and soon afterwards Providence came to our aid in a manner the possibility of which had never presented itself even to the sanguine imagination of Mr. Sears.

It lacked but two or three days of the completion of our lading when the little English trading steamer "Tubal Cain" came into port. Captain Savage, her commander, had been peddling his cargo at Balaklava and Kamiesh, and as Eupatoria was not very much out of his way to the Bosphorus, he came in here to dispose, if possible, of the balance of it and also to get a supply of coal.

Here then was an opportunity. I went on board and confided our condition to him, offering my services in aiding him to sell his goods to my friend, the Pasha, and moreover promising him an ample supply of coal on condition that he would take us in tow. He was only too glad to accept these terms. His stores were sold at once at a satisfactory profit, and he hauled alongside the next night to take in the coal. If Lord Dunraven had been there, his eagle eye would have detected a change of draught in the " Tubal Cain " on the following morning.

The barley being all on board, our sailing orders were received. I bade the unsuspicious Pasha good-bye as he overwhelmed me with thanks for the coal, and for the two cases of champagne, which I had already discovered was not forbidden by the Prophet.

When all the garrison had gone to sleep at their usual hour, we hove up our anchors simultaneously, the "Tubal Cain" taking us in tow. We had pleasant weather in the Black Sea, managed to enter the Bosphorus at night, and morning found us alongside of our dock.

Then Mr. Sears fairly jumped as he exclaimed, "That propeller ain't gone yet!" adding, "What's the use of a propeller, anyway?" It really did look as if we could get along pretty well without one; that is to say, in the Turkish employ; but if this sort of thing had happened in the French service, we might have lost a month's pay.

There was no difficulty in obtaining a spare screw from another steamer, which, with very little reaming, was made to fit on our shaft. As all the dock room was occupied by vessels of the navy, we were put to some little trouble after our cargo was discharged in moving all the ballast into the fore-peak and constructing a cofferdam around the stern of the ship. That having been pumped out, we hoisted our new propeller over it and put it upon the shaft. When this operation was completed, there was a final occasion for Mr. Sears to say, " The propeller ain't gone yet—and it never has been gone!" We had, by the exercise of no little prudence and ingenuity, fairly and honestly earned our charter money, for our employers had not been defrauded of a single piastre, although they did not know the difference between a steamer and a sailing vessel.

CHAPTER VII.

HAFIZ EFFENDI was an officer on duty at the arsenal with whom we were often associated in the routine of business. He was a man of agreeable manners, and always courteous in his deportment. He had been educated in Paris and had travelled extensively in England and in Germany. With the languages of those countries he was familiar, while he spoke French with the fluency of a native, and in his manners and habits was more a Frenchman than a Turk. He had never crossed the Atlantic, but it was his great desire and full intention at no distant day to visit the United States. Perhaps he attached himself to us for the purpose of getting all the information we could give him for the furtherance of his project, while he was always ready in return to answer our many questions about his own country, its government, its people and its resources.

The acquaintance thus formed in the line of his duties ripened into a sincere friendship upon which we set a value that it deserved. One day Hafiz asked the purser and myself to dine with him. He was still sufficient of a Turk to adhere in a degree to the customs of his country, for ladies were not included in the invitation. Indeed if it had been given, it could not have been accepted, as my family were then at Prinkipo, a charming island in the Sea of Marmora, not far distant from Constantinople, where they were out of the way of the rough associations they would have been obliged to encounter in the service in which we were now engaged.

We accordingly repaired to the house of our entertainer in Pera at the appointed hour of six o' clock, and were ushered into a reception-room which did not differ much in its furnishing from that we should have found at home. Our host soon presented himself in the conventional European and American evening dress, which we presumed had been donned for the occasion out of deference to his guests.

Dinner being announced soon afterwards, we were ushered into a dining-room of moderate dimensions, the walls on all sides covered with mirrors, giving us the impression that, as the Effendi was supposed generally to dine alone, he was fond of having himself for society all around, for he was really a very handsome man, worthy of being seen by himself as well as by others.

The *menu* was excellent but not elaborate, and did not differ much from what we might have found at a small dinner party at home, the only outlandish dishes on the table being the inevitable kobobs and a species of pillau. Of course there was some of the champagne not prohibited by the Prophet. We all had good appetites, and the dinner, as they say, "went off" in a very satisfactory manner.

After the last course, which did not include any sweets, Hafiz arose and said, " Now, gentlemen, we will adjourn to the drawing-room and take our coffee with the ladies." "You see," he added, with some slight hesitation, " our customs are not exactly like yours, and such as they are, I am innovating upon them somewhat in this instance. But my family will be glad to meet you, and I trust that you will find them agreeable."

He then ushered us into a large drawing-room, abounding also in mirrors, and elaborately furnished in semi-French and semi-Oriental style. The floor was carpeted with beautiful rugs; heavy curtains dropped before the windows, and divans, chairs and little tables were distributed around.

Reclining on the divans were four ladies, two of them in the bloom of youth, somewhere about sweet sixteen, one between her second and third decade, and another perhaps between her third and fourth. They were all beautiful women in their various stages of maturity, and their beauty was of various types.

Evidently variety was pleasing to the eye of our host, and although we had not the same interest in it that he had, it was pleasing to us. Of the two young houris, one might have sat for the portrait of Lolah and the other for that of Katinka. These two and the eldest (I mean the least youthful) were in Turkish costume exceedingly becoming, and the second in age, if it be permitted to apply that term to any of them, wore a *décolleté* European dress. The ease with which we made ourselves at home before this brilliant array was, I think, creditable to both of us, especially to my young friend, Mr. D——, who was a modest as well as a handsome youth, and he must have been regarded by these ladies as particularly handsome just then, when his face was suffused with blushes.

I have only given his initial, according to promise, for he is now a well known business man in New York, having achieved an honorable career. Hafiz might have been jealous, but if he was so, he gave no signs of any such disposition. We were not introduced to all of these ladies by name. Our host simply said, "*Voici ma famille.*" But he distinguished the lady in European dress as "*Ma femme Josephine.*" Now *femme* is a very convenient French word, and its ambiguity often serves a very desirable purpose.

Coffee and sweetmeats were passed around by a coal-black Nubian, and I will do Hafiz the credit to say that the coffee was brewed in French, and not in Turkish style. "The ladies will permit us to smoke," he said, as again he evinced his considerate politeness by offering us cigars, while he resorted to the chibook himself.

Then "*Ma femme Josephine*" gave us some excellent music, delicately touching the piano to accompany her songs which were a little after the style of Madame Yvette Guilbert.

After that I sat down by her side, while Hafiz was talking with the lady least young, having placed Mr. D—— between the brunette and blonde beauties, with whom he entered into an animated conversation, carried on chiefly by signs, for neither of the ladies spoke French or English, and "Evet" and "Yoke" (yes and no) was about all the Turkish the purser had at command.

Madame Josephine had no use for the words of one of her celebrated countrywomen, "God has given me my eyes, and I can provide the rest for myself." She certainly had a pair of soul-stirring eyes, abundant black hair, regular features, and a faultless form. To add to all this, she had been provided with a tongue tipped with sweetness and stirred with vivacity.

She was well read in French literature, especially conversant with the poetry of Racine, Corneille and Chénier, with the philosophy of Voltaire and the novels of the elder Dumas, and of Paul de Koch. Besides, she had studied English in the convent where she was educated, and when she got out of it she had seized upon Byron and Moore with avidity. She confessed that the pleasing scenes of Orientalism depicted by them had their influence in determining her life.

After a little preliminary talk on ordinary topics, she settled down to what she considered the chief object of a woman's existence, commencing with a romantic account of her own great affair of love.

"Ah, that dear Paris!" she exclaimed. "Hafiz has promised to take me there again when this terrible war is over." She said this in a tone sufficiently loud to attract his attention, and then added, "Will you not, *mon cher?*"

"Yes, certainly," he replied, with an approving smile. "You see," she said, turning towards me, "he is still under my control. Would you like to have me tell you of my first acquaintance with him?" "Nothing would interest me more," I replied, with all sincerity.

"Well, it was five years ago at the theatre when I was ravished by the divine Rachel in Adrienne. I was away from the world and from myself, till between the acts, an acquaintance brought Hafiz around to my box and presented him to me. Then I forgot Rachel, forgot

Adrienne, forgot myself, forgot everything! He simply looked at me, and I only looked at him. Nothing was said. It was all the language of the eyes. It was accomplished in an instant. It was *un coup d'éclair, une fureur, une tempête.* It was at once a beginning and an accomplished fact. Do they know what love means in America?"

Instead of a direct reply, I repeated these lines, that the situation brought to my remembrance.

> "Oh, love, sweet despot of the soul!
> Who would not own thy blest control?
> What's an eternity of power
> To love's enthralment for one hour?
> Who shall compare all worldly pelf,
> Fame or ambition, love of self,
> To the warm rapture of one kiss?
> That moment is an age of bliss!"

"Ah, monsieur," she replied, "you

have answered my question. Whoever
wrote those verses understood the meaning of the word. That is a good beginning for love, but one cannot always live in
a delirium. It would be exhausting. It is
natural as it is best for the hurricane to subside and for soft gentle zephyrs to succeed
it. That is a happier, because a more
permanent, condition. Thus it is now with
us. At that supreme moment we thought
that if we had each other we should never
want anything more, but now some accessories are convenient." And she cast a
sly glance across the room. "For my
part, I have music, books, dress, jewelry,
a carriage, and everything that I desire.
We love each other still, but more sensibly." Upon my saying that with all the
surroundings that made her happy she
must sometimes find Constantinople dull
after Paris, she assented; but continued,

"Well, we are going there again for a little excitement, and when we return I think I shall be quite contented. But I am about to tell you what followed that grand *coup* at the theatre. I did not ask Hafiz if he was already married, nor did he ask me any foolish questions. We loved, and that was sufficient. I wished to prove his love, although I did not doubt it, and so I told him that we must be married in a church. He consented. I knew he would, as I would have been willing to have been married in a mosque. I adore Lalla Rookh; don't you? Do you remember what Hinda said to Hafed?

"'Thou for my sake at Allah's shrine,
And I—at *any* God's for thine!'"

Well, I am still a Catholic; I go to mass sometimes, but I don't go to confession here, for I have no sins to confess. This kind of life is so quiet that there is no temptation or opportunity to sin. Do you think Byron was a very *mauvais sujet?*" I told her I did not think he was so bad as he painted himself. "I'll tell you what I think about him," she replied. "He was a bad man for an Englishman. As a Frenchman he would not have been bad. In England they place religion before love. In France love is supreme over religion and everything else."

Our host perhaps thought that this conversation had lasted long enough. He walked over to where we were sitting, and said, but not in a tone of reproach, "*Ma femme*, you have been talking a great deal about yourself and me." Josephine turned her beautiful eyes upon him and replied, in a voice devoid of all affectation, "What else could I talk about but that which interests me most?" And I saw by the glance he returned, that she was still

"His Nourmahal, his harem's light."

Then we had some more music, and the two youngest ladies each executed a *pas seul*. They did not dance with their feet, but swayed voluptuously to and fro, keeping time to the music with this silent music of their own. At last the delightful evening came to an end, and we bade adieu to Hafiz Effendi and his charming family. Most charming of all was "*Ma femme Josephine.*"

CHAPTER VIII.

Two days afterwards I was sent for from the Arsenal. News had been received from Eupatoria that there was the probability of a Russian attack upon the garrison; that many of the soldiers had died and were dying of typhoid fever; that provisions were again becoming scarce, and that supplies of men and food were in urgent demand.

This time I found old Mustapha very much awake. He had laid aside his chibook, uncoiled himself, got up from the divan, and was pacing the floor in a state of actual excitement. Then came the usual question, " Have you got your coal?" sharply put. "No, your Excellency, it has been promised but it has not yet come." He gave an order to an official attendant in an angry tone, and then turned to me saying, "Your coal will come this afternoon, and to-night you will take on board one thousand men and five hundred sheep, and sail to-morrow morning for Eupatoria."

I was about to make some remonstrance when he waved his hand impatiently as a signal for me to take my leave, which I did forthwith, and repaired on board to communicate the intelligence to Mr. Sears.

He received it with an extended whistle and then observed, "Well, I thought these Turkish ways were too good to last. We've had an easy time of it so far, but this is crowdin' the mourners, I should say. Why, the Frenchmen never'd have done anything like this."

Then he took his log-slate out of the drawer and sat down to make figures. He knew every inch of room there was in the ship from frequent experience in the stowage of men, cattle and cargo, and he now made his calculations accordingly.

After a while he arrived at this result: "Allowin' two square foot for a man, and providin' the sodjers will stand up all the way, and calling every sheep a sodjer, providin' he will stand on his hind legs, we can just about accommodate 'em. Sheep won't do that, though. The sodjers will take up all the room in the between decks and on deck, and the sheep will have to go on top o' one another in the hold. Why didn't the P'shaw have 'em killed and skun, so't they could go as mutton? A good many of them will be mutton anyway before they get there."

I remarked that it was too late to adopt that expedient, and if there had been time for it the Pasha was not in a state of mind to entertain the suggestion. "'Pears to me," answered Sears, "from the way you say he looked and acted so different from usual, this Eupatoria business wasn't enough to stir him up so. Somethin' or 'nother must have happened to home. That's what comes of having large families."

"Very likely," I said, "but that does not concern us. The question is, can we carry all these troops and sheep?" "No, sir, we can't," replied Sears, "but I suppose we've got to. It's fated that way."

The coal came alongside in the afternoon, and in the course of the evening the sheep were driven down the dock and put into the hold. And, before morning, we received our complement of men, so that we were ready to cast off and go to sea soon after daylight.

Some idea of the appearance of the ship may be formed by looking at a Coney Island steamboat as she leaves the wharf on a warm Sunday morning. The officer in command of the regiment, answering in rank to our term of Colonel, bitterly remonstrated against this excessive overcrowding. I told him we were obeying the Pasha's orders, and that I should be greatly obliged if he would address his remonstrances to him. Whereupon he made a significant gesture by squeezing his throat with his fingers, that was very suggestive of what might happen if he should presume to interfere, and remarked with becoming resignation, " God is great, His will be done." " Jes' so, jes' so," observed Mr. Sears.

We threaded our way down the Golden

Horn among the fleet, rounded Seraglio Point, and pointed up the Bosphorus against a strong head-wind which veered to the eastward when we got into the Black Sea, where we rolled about in the trough of the waves, and there was a condition of seasickness among the soldiers too abominably filthy to be commented upon.

We had proceeded in this way about three hours when we made a sail ahead. As we drew near to her she proved to be a small Xebec, partially dismasted and flying a signal of distress. Coming up with her, we saw that her deck was crowded with men and women, frantically waving their arms and shrieking at the top of their voices. Upon being hailed by the interpreter, they reported that they were in a sinking condition and wished to abandon their vessel. They were from Sukumkale, bound to Constantinople, and had been blown out of their course by a south-westerly gale, had lost their mainmast, and had sprung a leak that was steadily gaining upon them in spite of their pumps.

Of course there was nothing to be done but to lower a lifeboat and take them off. The cool-headed old Sears volunteered for this duty, and in two trips got them all safely on board.

There were twenty-six in all: eight men of the crew, seventeen female passengers, and a nondescript. Every one, especially every woman, was in such a state of fright that they were nearly crazy. The women were more frightened, if possible, when they got on board the steamer than they were at the prospect of perishing in the sea. They screamed and cowered down under the bulwarks of the quarter-deck as the crowd of savage soldiers pressed in upon them, so that I was obliged to organize our whole crew as a marine guard, armed with capstan-bars, heavers, belaying-pins, and whatever came to hand to keep them off. Fortunately, the arms and ammunition of the troops were stowed away aft under the cabin.

The military officers were too seasick and too cowardly to control the mob. Although an agony of fear distorted the features of these poor girls, their exquisite beauty shone through their tears. Some of them were of the Persian type, with lustrous black hair falling over their shoulders, dark eyes and silken lashes; others, and these the majority, with brown or golden hair, large blue eyes and complexions like a peach when the dew of the morning is upon it. There they crouched down upon the deck, their beautiful heads resting upon the breasts of each other in the vain endeavor to conceal their charms.

"What are we going to do with these hell-cats?" asked the practical Mr. Sears. "If somethin' ain't done they'll jump overboard, and I dunno but what that's about the best thing they can do."

"Get them down below as soon as possible," I said. "Whereabouts?" inquired Sears. "The cabin's full o' them Turkish officers, and that's the only place there is."

"Well, get the officers out and the women in."

Sears jumped below, calling two or three men of the marine guard after him, and in a few moments he got the officers out, in spite of their objections, for they were too seasick to offer much resistance. Leaving the doctor at the door as a sentinel to prevent them from re-entering, he put his head out of the companionway, calling out: "All clear, sir. If you'll get the women along with that old nigger that 'pears to have 'em in charge, I'll shut 'em all up together."

By means of the interpreter they were made to understand what disposition was to be made of them, and the sunshine of their eyes beamed through the mist of their tears as they followed the "nigger" down below. Then Sears locked the door and put the key in his pocket, having stationed the doctor as a sentinel.

The cursing and growling of those who had been so summarily turned out of their quarters was loud and deep. The officers and soldiers all had a right to be angry, but the man against whom their anger should have been directed was doubtless smoking his chibook and sipping his coffee, squatted on his divan, and more sleepy than ever after the excitement of the previous day had passed off.

For them there was no sleep to be had, unless they got it perpendicularly; and as it was impossible to do very much cooking for such a multitude, their only provisions were soup, hard-tack and water. Two nights were to be passed on board, under the conditions of the weather, before we could reach Eupatoria. Mr. Sears, the purser and I were discussing the situation, when we were joined by the chief engineer, who reported that one of his firemen, a Maltese, who understood Turkish perfectly well, had told him that there was a very ugly feeling among the soldiers on account of their limited accommodations and rations, and of their rough handling by the crew since our new passengers had come on board, and he did not know what might come of it.

I was not surprised to hear this, for I suspected it already. "I'm cur'ous to know what they propose to do about it," said Sears. "Here we be, and with the doctor, the only five white men, as you may say, on the ship, the crew bein' mainly Frenchmen and the passengers Turks. S'posin' it's fated that they should kill us, they couldn't navigate the ship, and they don't know enough to bile water to keep the ingines a-goin'; but it ain't fated that way. They're too seasick to do anything. They won't do nothin' anyway till we git in, and we'd better be kind of careful then how we circulate 'round ashore till they get their bellies full once more and so get good-natured.

"In the meantime," he asked, "as the staysail and trysails have been keeping her tolerably steady lately, hadn't we better take 'em in and let her roll again so's to keep their stomachs out of order ? If that ain't enough, perhaps the doctor might put a little tartar emetic in the soup."

The purser had no suggestions to offer; his mind was probably wandering to the drawing-room of Hafiz Effendi, and I must confess that I would not have been sorry to be there to.

Our colloquy was interrupted by the cry of " Sail ho!" from the lookout at the masthead. " Where away ? " I asked. " Right ahead, sir." " Can you make her out ? " " Yes, sir ; she is square-rigged, under easy sail, and coming this way." In a short time we could see her from the deck, and it was not long before we could distinguish a ship under single reefed topsails, a pennant streaming from her mainroyal truck, and the British ensign floating from her peak.

She was evidently in no hurry; but in order to make sure that she would heave to, I ordered our ensign to be hoisted half-mast and Union down, and the Turkish flag at the fore. This had the desired effect, and her main topsail was immediately laid to the mast. We slowed down to barely steerage way and ranged alongside within speaking distance, waiting, according to etiquette, for the first hail to come from the frigate, as it did.

"What steamer is that?" "The William Penn, bound for Eupatoria." "Are you in distress?"

"I will come on board, if you please, and inform you."

"Very well."

The quarter-boat was lowered, and taking with me some late English newspapers that I knew would be most acceptable, I was soon alongside and up the ladder of the frigate, where I was met by an officer at the gangway, and escorted to the Captain on the quarter-deck.

He was a somewhat elderly man, with a rosy complexion, a kindly eye, and the traditional mutton-chop whiskers. He received me very courteously, extending his hand, and saying that he would be very happy to be of service if I would tell him what we needed.

"It is a rather long story, sir," I said, "but I will try to cut it as short as I can. First, however, let me give you these newspapers, which you would like to have, as they must be later than any that you have seen."

"Thanks, they will be very welcome," he replied. "Now, will you step down into my cabin?"

As we entered it he called to his servant, "Sherry, two glasses and biscuits."

These were at once produced, and we sat down at the table. "Now, we'll take a glass of wine and then you go ahead," said the old Captain.

As succinctly as possible I told him how abominably overcrowded we were forced to be when we left Constantinople, and then gave him an account of the addition we had received a few hours before.

To all of this he listened with attention and manifest interest, frequently interupting my narrative with, "Bless my soul; you don't say so!" and the like. He touched the bell for his servant, and said: "Put another glass upon the table, and then say to the First Lieutenant that I should like to see him if he is disengaged."

The Lieutenant came down at once and I was presented to him. "Thorton," said the Captain, in the customary familiar style of the navy when off duty, "here is a Yankee skipper in trouble—Bless my soul, sir," he said, turning to me, " pray excuse my rudeness, I did not mean it; I should have said an American Captain." " No apology is necessary, sir," I replied. " I am rather proud of the title ; you were quite right. In the merchant service we are called Captains by courtesy amongst ourselves, but by the officers of our navy, as well as of yours, we are frequently called masters, or skippers, if you please."

" Thank you for taking it so pleasantly," he replied, " but it was rude in me nevertheless. Let's take another glass of sherry." If Salisbury and Olney had only had a glass of sherry between them, it would have done more than all their diplomatic correspondence to settle the Venezuela dispute.

At the Captain's request I repeated my story to the First Lieutenant as concisely as I could, for time was valuable to me if it was not so to them. When I had finished it the Captain proposed the familiar question, " What are you going to do about it ? "

" I came on board, sir," I replied, " to see what *you* were going to do about it."

" What *can* we do about it ? " he rejoined.

" You can do a great deal, sir," I said. " We have saved these women and men from drowning, and I would not greatly care if the men had been drowned, but the women ! Gentlemen, I wish you could have seen them as they are penned up in a small cabin to hide them from the eyes of a thousand infuriated brutes who are threatening us with mutiny; and whose officers, turned out of their cabins to take their chance with them on the crowded deck, are making no attempt to control them. Won't you take these poor wretches on board? If this wind holds you will be in the Bosphorus to-night, and you can bundle them all ashore at Buyukdere."

The Captain and the Lieutenant agreed that carrying passengers would be entirely contrary to the rules of Her Majesty's service.

"I know," I replied, "what Her Gracious Majesty, God bless her, if she were here present, what every woman in England and America would think, and what every man would say." "What would they say?" asked the Captain. "Damn the rules of the service," I replied, "when it is a question of humanity."

It was a bold speech, but it had its effect. The two naval officers looked silently at each other for a moment, and then the Captain brought his fist down on the table in a style that made the decanter and glasses rattle, as he said to his Lieutenant, "Call away the pinnace, sir, and have those people brought on board."

I thanked him from the bottom of my heart. "No thanks," he said, "you are right; take another glass of sherry and we will go on deck and see this thing out."

I there bade him good-bye and was hastening to the gangway to get down into my boat, when he put his hand on my shoulder and said, "But won't you stop to introduce us to the ladies?"

"Thank you, no," I replied; "you can introduce yourselves to them, as we did, and I am sure they will be more pleased to see you than they were to see us."

The pinnace was already alongside the steamer when I reached the gangway. "Now, Mr. Sears," I said, "you can take the interpreter down to the cabin, unlock the door, and tell him to inform that colored gentleman and his protegées that they are to be transferred to that man-of-war, now on her way to Constantinople. Get them up as soon as possible, and down the ladder into the Englishman's boat, then pitch their crew in after them."

Never was Sears more active than he was in executing this order. The pinnace was soon alongside of the frigate, and we saw the bedraggled crowd passed up a gangway ladder, and the boat hoisted in.

Then, as her maintopsail was filled, we hoisted our ensign and saluted by running it up and down three times, the courtesy being returned. In a moment her yards were covered with men shaking out the reefs, loosing the light sails, and rigging out the studdingsail booms. In less than five minutes she was under a cloud of canvas, and, as she careened slightly to starboard, her bright copper was awash, and, with a bone in her mouth, she spread away to the south.

"Look at that, look at that!" exclaimed Sears in an ecstasy of delight. "That's a sight for the eyes of an old sailor. There she goes, without any bilers or blacksmith work to push her along. See her spread out her own white wings like a bird of the air! God made the birds and He learned men to imitate 'em. The devil learned men to build steamboats, and helped 'em out with his own hell-fire."

Having exhausted himself in this burst of enthusiasm he subsided into his usual taciturnity. The frigate was, indeed, a picture to look at, as she clothed herself in canvas, and not a voice was heard, and no sound came from her, but that of the boatswain's whistle.

Never again will there be exhibited such seamanship as that of those days. The poetry of the ocean has given place to prosaic utility, as the beauty of the sailing ship is now superseded by the downright ugliness of the ironclad, and "whitewinged messengers of commerce" are fast disappearing and giving place to the black leviathans that monopolize war and trade.

Even with the few that remain, the double topsail rig, and the three, four, and five-masted schooners, are sad departures from the perfect symmetry of the olden type. Soon there will be nothing left but the disproportionate playthings of our grown-up boys.

The sailor has gone and the blacksmith has come. In naval war it is now only a question of rams and torpedoes, of guns that can penetrate any armor, of armor that is impervious to any guns, with crews of coal-passers, deck-hands and gunners, hammering away till one or the other goes to the bottom with her thousand men. Our merchant marine is gone, but we do not feel the need of it as our fathers did, when merchant Captains like Hull, Decatur, Perry, Bainbridge, Truxton, and McDonough, with crews brought up in the merchant service, gained their victories more by splendid seamanship than by the training of guns.

Mr. Sears came down from his poetic exaltation, and busied himself with having the cabin cleansed so that the officers might again occupy the quarters from which he had so rudely ejected them. They had measurably recovered from their sea-sickness, and their appetites came to them as they were domesticated once more. The best that we had was spread before them; soup, sardines, potted meats, preserves, and the champagne that the Prophet did not forbid. They made a hearty meal, and the Colonel, who was a very good fellow at heart, especially when his heart was warmed up by champagne, then went on deck, at my request, and made a conciliatory speech to the soldiers. He told them that the ship was overcrowded on account of a misapprehension on shore of her capacity; that they must bear their sufferings in consequence of it like true followers of the Prophet, and that there would be a constant supply of soup to the full ability of the coppers to turn it out.

For this purpose some of the sheep were killed, and their ears were saved. This was with the consent of the special supercargo having them in charge. He was to see that the five hundred sheep were delivered at Eupatoria : if any died on the passage he was to cut off their ears in order to account for the missing. He might have sold a hundred if the opportunity had been offered him. The whole of his duty was to produce the sheep, or the ears of sheep that were not delivered.

So passed the night, and another day and another night, hammering against a head sea; and it was bitterly cold as the snow flew over the decks, and the men crouched down as best they could for sleep while their officers were very comfortable in the cabin.

On the afternoon of the second day we arrived at our destined port, and were as glad to get rid of our passengers, as they were to go ashore. The delivery of the sheep as stated in the log-book was 405 alive, 190 ears, equal to 95 sheep, total 500. A few of them had gone into the soup, but most of the 95 had been smothered or trampled to death in the hold.

CHAPTER IX.

THE reinforcement of troops we had brought up was entirely unnecessary. The Pasha had not asked for them. On the contrary, they were very unwelcome, as just so many more men were to be fed. It was an unfounded rumor that had produced the scare at Constantinople. The Russians had not the remotest idea of regaining Eupatoria at present, for they knew that they could not hold it against the fleet of the allies that would bombard it, and they now had no ships of their own to resist them.

The possession of the place would have been as useless to them as it was to the Turks, and so they were content to let them keep their white elephant. "I wish," said our old friend, "that you had brought us up a full cargo of provisions and coal instead. The sheep are more welcome than the troops."

The weather in February was still as cold as when we were here before. The little coal we had been able to supply from our bunkers was nearly exhausted, and the champagne the Prophet did not forbid was all gone. His "brother and his friend," as he called me, was only too happy to turn over to him again all the coal that could be spared, and two more cases of champagne, for all of which the "brother and friend" will candidly acknowledge that he expected there would be some value received.

One would suppose that we had an abundance of champagne for any emergency, and so we had. In the beginning of the war a large quantity of it shipped to Odessa had been captured *in transitu* and sold at auction at an exceedingly low price. I bought one hundred cases of Veuve Cliquot at five dollars per case as a speculation, intending to sell it again at a large profit; but I concluded that the most advantageous disposition of it was to give much of it away. It was accordingly stored at a warehouse and drawn upon as occasion required. It was the best investment that could have been made.

The mistake of Mustapha Pasha was not, however, quite so costly as that made at an earlier period by an Englishman, whose countrymen made so many notorious blunders during the war, this among the rest.

In November, 1855, General Vivian was in command of the British forces stationed at Kertch, and General Shirley commanded the Turkish contingent, idling away the time at Buyukdere, where he found it rather dull. In one of his letters to his old friend Vivian, after discussing military affairs, he added something about his family, who were likewise tired of the monotony. In return he received a short note to this effect, " Bring everybody up here; they will be most welcome."

Shirley had forgotten that he had mentioned his family in his despatch, and jumped to the conclusion that the Russians were threatening Kertch with an attack, and that reinforcements were urgently needed, whereas the sole intention of General Vivian was to give him, his wife and the young ladies an outing. So he embarked his three thousand cavalry on board a fleet of sailing vessels that were taken in tow by steamers, and away they all went across the Black Sea to Kertch.

When General Vivian saw this fleet coming up the Straits he had no idea from whence it had sailed or whether it was friend or foe. His anxiety, however, was soon relieved by Shirley's jumping ashore and hailing him with, "How are you, old boy? You see me here."

"Yes," answered Vivian, "I was expecting you, but what the devil is the meaning of this fleet?"

"Why, it has brought up my cavalry, to be sure," was the reply.

"Your cavalry! Bless your soul, there isn't a thing for a horse to eat here and I don't need any help."

An explanation followed. The result was that Shirley's visit was a short one. The ships discharged neither men nor horses, but weighed anchor as soon as they had watered, and returned with the cavalry to Buyukdere, from whence they had come.

The Pasha at Eupatoria did not exactly follow this example, but he was disposed to send back a thousand invalids in place of the recruits, until he was made by the coal and champagne to realize that we could furnish accommodations for only three hundred men of that class. This number was accordingly sent on board and properly cared for. They were in a deplorable condition, and it was not surprising that several of them died on the passage.

In the case of the French soldiers who died, the burial always took place at sea, but this was never consented to by the Turks, if it could possibly be avoided. In the present instance their feelings could be respected, and the bodies were retained on board till arrival, as the weather was cold.

Mr. Sears observed that "they would keep very well if stowed under the to'gallant forc'sle out of the way of the sun." When the first was brought on deck, he stood looking at his face for a moment and then remarked, "I've seen a good many dead Frenchmen, but this is the first dead Turk I've set my eyes on. I wonder where he's gone."

Sears was a believer in phrenology, a science that has an intimate relation to his favorite doctrine of fatalism. He stooped down and felt his bumps, and then turning to the purser, whom he knew to be a staunch Presbyterian, he remarked, "Reverence is pretty large, so I hope he's gone to heaven; but their heaven ain't the same as our'n, with halos and crowns and harps and hosannas and hallelujahs and such, is it, Mr. D.?" "No," replied the purser. "Their idea of heaven is very different from ours; it is a sensual heaven, with gardens, trees, flowers, music, dancing and——" "Must be kind o' pleasant," interjected Sears. "Yes," continued the purser, "for those who have no higher aspirations than to live in gardens with houris." "With what!" exclaimed the philosopher; "what are houris?" "Houris," was the reply, "are supposed to be women somewhat like those you called hell-cats the other day." Sears shook his head meditatively and said, "Well, I reckon our kind o' heaven may be a little dull and monotonous like, but on the whole I'd rather put up with it than go to their'n. Bend on to him, Bo'sn; take him for'ard and cover him up. Eight bells! Lay aft, two of you, and heave the log."

On arrival I learned that the Englishman had not landed his passengers at Buyukdere, as I had suggested, but had taken them directly down to Constantinople and turned them over to Mustapha Pasha. When I made my usual report at the arsenal, I found him coiled up again in his customary place on the divan and in his habitual mood of silence and self-satisfaction. After the questions to which I had become accustomed, "When did you arrive?" and "Have you got your coal?" had been answered, I asked: "Did your Excellency receive some shipwrecked people we picked up on the way to Eupatoria?" He nodded his head in assent. "What became of them?" I inquired. Mustapha evidently thought that this was none of my business, for his reply was very short: "They were—confiscated."

Comment has been made upon the bad

management of the English commissariat at Balaklava that entailed such disastrous consequences. The only excuses made for it were an ignorance of the country and the distance from the seat of war. The Turks had not these apologies to offer for the neglect of their troops at Eupatoria. That station was within less than two days' sail from Constantinople and easily supplied with all the necessaries required.

The place was captured by the allies without any resistance in November, 1854, and was strongly fortified on the land side against attack from the enemy, should they be disposed to regain it, as they were when, in the winter that ensued, they made an unsuccessful attempt in that direction. It is said, upon authority, which seems scarcely credible, that the failure of the Russian troops in this instance had such an effect upon the Czar that he died of chagrin soon after receiving the news.

The only object the allies could have had in possessing themselves of this insignificant port must have been to obtain a base of supplies from the rich farming country in the interior. For a time this scheme worked admirably; the natives were almost always ready to sell their produce to these new and eager customers, and when they were indisposed to do so, foraging parties obtained all they desired without cost. There was no let or hindrance to this generally beneficial commerce till Mentchikoff withdrew a large part of his force from Sebastopol, for the purpose of harassing his enemies from the outside and of eventually driving them into the sea, as he ineffectually attempted to do in the battles of Inkerman and Balaklava.

Although he was not successful in this, he did accomplish the shutting off their means of obtaining provisions, and kept the road open for abundantly supplying his own troops in the field, as well as the beleaguered garrison at Sebastopol. Eupatoria had been left mainly in charge of the Turks and a few companies of French soldiers, and it had been left to starve.

My "friend and brother," Azim Pasha, had remonstrated as far as he dared, in vain, and he and his troops hungered and froze with resignation, rather welcoming than deploring the sickness that was daily depleting their ranks, as it reduced the number of mouths to be fed.

It suited us very well to lie at the dock in Constantinople and draw our pay for doing nothing, but humanity prompted me to induce Hafiz Effendi to stir up old

Mustapha to the performance of some part of his duty.

"The best thing you can do for those poor devils up there," I said, "is to send them provisions instead of more troops. There is no danger of any further attack from the Russians, who don't want the place any more than you ought to want to retain it. They need fuel to warm them and food to eat. Fill our hold with coal and our between decks with groceries and provisions; give us a deck load of sheep and hay, and send us off as quickly as you can."

The Effendi accordingly awakened Mustapha and kept his eyes open long enough for him to sign an order to this effect, and away we sped to Eupatoria to gladden the hearts of the sufferers. My friend and brother, who was by this time again out of coal, and champagne, received me with open arms. He would be no longer obliged to cover himself with human comforters and to confine himself to hard-tack and cold water, but he could keep his house warm, treat himself to a cup of coffee, cover himself with sheepskins that were as acceptable as the mutton that had been under them, to say nothing of an occasional sip of the champagne that the Prophet did not forbid. The remainder of our service under the Turks may be summarized as repetitions of trips like this with provisions for Eupatoria, and returning with invalids.

The news of peace being declared reached us on the 2d day of April, 1856. The event had been anticipated for a long time, and, in business parlance, had been discounted by all the belligerents who, excepting the English, had come to the wise conclusion that it was folly to sacrifice any more lives in useless warfare.

The English were opposed to a speedy termination of hostilities, while the French were anxious to bring them to a close. The *élan* with which they had gone into the war had long since subsided. On the other hand, the mistakes the English had made, and their suffering in consequence of them, had taught them some salutary lessons. In short, it may be said that at this period the French had become tired and demoralized, whereas the English, with bull-dog pertinacity, had just got themselves into good fighting trim. The French were ready to leave off; the English were ready to begin afresh. The news was therefore hailed with joy by the French, and received by the English as a bitter pill that Napoleon obliged them to swallow.

He knew full well the conditions to which each party had arrived, that the superiority of his troops could no longer be maintained, and that if any more victories were to be won, the English would be entitled to the credit. From first to last his army had not only been fighting the Russians, but it had been engaged in humiliating the English, and this process was as much a source of satisfaction to him as were his victories over the common enemy.

The land forces of the French being the most numerous, their generals naturally exercised a greater control. This was made manifest in things both great and small. It was a luxury for the French to supply the deficient commissariat of the English, and it was their policy to place them at disadvantage in battle, as they did in the culminating event of the war, when, as has been already related, the English were repulsed at the Redan, while the French triumphantly scaled the Malakoff. French and English alike held the Turks in derision. All three of them had a greater respect for the Russians than for each other.

But the British navy did excite the admiration and envy of the French. They learned some useful lessons in seamanship from their association with it. But it was in vain that their ships endeavored to rival those of the English in naval tactics and evolutions.

It must not be forgotten that 1855 was still the era of sailing ships in the navies as well as in the mercantile marines of the world—a surviving era of a now almost forgotten seamanship. It was a study to see an English and French line-of-battle ship or frigate coming to anchor together. On board the former, silently and as if by magic, every sail was furled at once before the Frenchmen could man their yards and gather up the bunts, chattering all the while like a lot of magpies, and all apparently giving orders to each other. Happily for the French, they are now on more even terms, as seamanship is no longer required.

There is a general impression that the introduction of iron-clads commenced with the plating of the Merrimac and the building of the Monitor. This is not true, for there was a rude beginning made by the English in this war.

Two iron-clads were sent out from England in tow, although they had limited steam-power of their own. They were wooden vessels plated over with iron sheets not more than an inch thick, with open bulwarks, and decks rounded up so that a shell might roll into the water in case it did not immediately explode.

They floated almost as low as rafts. At the reduction of Kinbourn the masts were taken out of them and they were towed as far as it was prudent for the tugs to accompany them, and then they propelled themselves under the batteries which they successfully silenced.

I do not know what became of them afterwards, or if they were ever again brought into requisition. They have probably been broken up long ago, but they should have been preserved to appear in future naval exhibits where they would attract as much attention alongside of a modern battle-ship as did the first railroad engine by the side of one of the latest construction at the World's Fair in Chicago.

The navy played but a small part in

the Crimean War. Almost its only use was to prevent the exit of the Russian fleet from Sebastopol, which would have been disastrous to the seaports in its neighborhood occupied by the Allies, and to the transports that brought their supplies of men, munitions and provisions.

As to the Russian fleet, it had accomplished its purpose of annihilating that of the Turks at Sinope before the Allies made their appearance in the Black Sea. After that, it retired to the harbor of Sebastopol to await the course of events. When the fortune of war at last went against the Russians, as we have seen, their ships were scuttled and sunk.

In bringing this narrative of personal experiences and of the great events to which they were incident *quorum parva pars fui*, to a close, the writer may be permitted to chronicle succinctly his own conclusions. They may not be those of the historian, the statesman or the politician. They claim no such authority. They simply emanate from the quarter-deck of an American transport steamer.

The Allies certainly succeeded in curbing Russia's designs upon Turkey and in postponing the inevitable for a time. The life of the "sick man" has been prolonged forty years, but the sick man is bound sooner or later to die. The question is, whether it would not have been better for the world if he had yielded up the ghost in 1854, when Nicholas diagnosed his case and said to the British ambassador at his court in almost so many words, "Leave him to me; you shall have Egypt, and I will guarantee you that, and your Indian possessions, for all time."

England knew that she could not make

a better bargain for herself than this, provided it could have been carried out. But unfortunately for her, the star of the third Napoleon was at that time in the ascendant.

It was a mean estimate of him that was made after the day of Sedan to say that "he went up like a rocket and came down like a stick." He did go up like a rocket, but he stayed up in the zenith of his splendor and power for twenty years. England feared him before the Crimean War, during the war, and for a long time afterwards. All Europe was afraid of him; and we, too, were a little afraid of him ourselves, during our family quarrel.

Now that he has gone and the inordinate pride of France has been somewhat humbled, perhaps there may soon be a reconstruction of the map of the eastern continent, and the second Nicholas may invite England to accede to his terms. If this should come to pass, I can only commend to my good friends, the Turks, whom I shall always hold in kindly remembrance, a graceful submission to their own doctrine of fatalism, which Mr. Sears was wont to consider their crowning virtue.

THE END.

www.ingramcontent.com/pod-product-compliance
Lightning Source LLC
Chambersburg PA
CBHW020924230426
43666CB00008B/1559